A GREAT WEEKEND
IN PARIS

A GREAT WEEKEND

IN **PARIS**

"Paris…? You're going to Paris…?" There's always a hint of envy and nostalgia in the voices of those who stay behind. Indeed, few cities in the world can claim the beauty and charm of Paris. On each street corner, it seems, an artist was born, a writer once lived. And the history of the country itself unfolded in Paris. No other site is so closely linked to the national memory. Despite attempts at decentralisation, the political decisions of France are still made in Paris, and all the latest trends—frivolous or enduring—in fashion, philosophy and art radiate begin in Paris.

Everywhere you walk in the City of Lights will take you through a charmed neighbourhood. People come from the four corners of the earth to see Paris. And everyone sees something a bit different. The majestic and miniscule streets reveal the marvels of the past like sumptuous decors which reflect a time when every construction, large or small, was meant to be a masterpiece.

You have to be in a curious mood to explore Paris. Look up: at the corner of a street you can admire the turret of a Renaissance townhouse; follow the curving lines of a Rococo wrought-iron balcony; or the scrolls on an Art Nouveau window frame. Don't just window-shop; push open the doors of the lovely shops to see the treasures within. Take time to observe the shimmering light reflected off the Seine onto the stone buildings of Île Saint-Louis, then stop in front of a relief sculpture highlighted by the slanting rays of the sun.

This city is anything but an inanimate decor. Quite the contrary: hurried and stressed Parisians rush past this lovely backdrop, yet do find time to enjoy the urban lifestyle both during the day and at night. Restaurants and brasseries, cafés and bistro terraces are all favourite meeting places, starting early in the morning with a *petit noir* until late at night, for a last drink.

Paris is the epicentre of innovation. It produces, inspires and nourishes an immense market devoted to the arts, fashion, decoration and new styles. Architects, interior decorators and designers compete to create unique, sophisticated boutiques, galleries and shops. And the show doesn't stop there: go in any of these Parisian shops; you won't be disappointed.

If you're looking for a pair of shoes, a household item, a handbag, a scarf or an odd piece of fabric, or merely want to experience some of the charms of Paris without buying anything, you'll find what you're looking for and perhaps a few things you didn't know you needed.

No matter what your style, just follow your intuition and explore. Let yourself be guided by the city itself.

"You're going to Paris?... What luck!..."

Who said, *"Paris will always be Paris?"*

Getting there

Paris is a major European hub, and there are a multitude of ways to get there. Here's an overview of the many ways to reach the City of Lights.

BY PLANE

Paris has two airports: Orly (15 kilometres to the south) and Roissy Charles-de-Gaulle (30 kilometres to the north). Flights from Strasbourg, Toulouse, Lyon, Marseille, Nice, Bordeaux, Brest and Clermont-Ferrand arrive at Orly. Most international flights land at Roissy CDG. The following airlines have regular flights to Paris:

Air Canada, 10, Rue de la Paix, 75002 Paris ☎ 01.44.50.20.20.

Air France, 119, Champs-Élysées, 75008, and **Air Inter Europe** ☎ 0 802.802.802.

British Airways, 12, Rue Castiglione, 75001 Paris ☎ 0 802 802 902.

British Midland, 4, Place de Londres, Roissy-en-France, 95700 ☎ 01.48.62.55.65.

Delta Airlines, 4, Rue Scribe, 75009 ☎ 01.47.68.92.92.

United Airlines, 55, Rue Raspail, 92532 Levallois Perret ☎ 0800.01.913.

GETTING TO PARIS FROM THE AIRPORT

From Roissy CDG: The Roissy-Rail service goes to the Gare de Nord train station, to Luxembourg and to Denfert-Rochereau in about 35 minutes (departures every 10 minutes, 4:30am-11:30pm; approximately 47 francs). The *Roissybus* service links Roissy to the Opera in about 45 minutes (departures every 15 minutes from 5:45am to 11pm; 45 francs). The RATP buses 350 and 351 leave for the Gare du Nord or the Place de la Nation approximately every 30 minutes (50-minute trip, depending on traffic). The

Air France bus (5:30-11pm) goes from Roissy to the Palais des Congrès (at the Porte Maillot), or to the Étoile, with departures every 20 minutes (45-65 francs). A taxi costs about 250 francs to the city centre, but the price also depends on the time, in other words, the traffic. Add 5 francs per suitcase.

From Orly Ouest or Sud: Take the automated *Orlyval* to Antony, then change to the RER line B, which operates from

6:30am to 9:15pm (46-57 francs). *Orlyrail* (bus shuttle, then RER line C) takes about 40 minutes, with departures every 15 minutes, from 5:30am to 11:15pm (28-32 francs). It will stop at all the stations within the city limits. *Orlybus* is a direct bus service that goes to

CHANNEL CROSSINGS

Travel between France and England has never been easier since the opening of the tunnel under the English channel.

If you want to drive your car, *Le Shuttle* is an easy and comfortable way to go; the trip takes only 35 minutes. The drive from Calais to Paris then takes about three hours.

The *Eurostar* links Waterloo station in London to the Gare de Nord in Paris in just three hours. You have a choice of up to 14 trains per day. Discounts are available for those under 26 years of age, for children, for seniors and for groups. There are also a number of ferry companies, with frequent crossings from Dover to Calais (about 80 minutes), from Portsmouth to St-Malo (nine hours), and from Portsmouth to Le Havre (six hours). Hovercrafts speed from Dover to Calais, and a catamaran crosses from Folkestone to Boulogne.

Denfert-Rochereau. It operates from 6am to 11pm, every 15 minutes (30 francs).
The Air France bus, which

goes from Orly to the Invalides, stops at the Porte d'Orléans, at Montparnasse and at Duroc (32 francs). A taxi from Orly will cost about 150 francs to the city centre (depending on traffic), with an additional 5 francs per suitcase.

BY TRAIN

Depending on where you start from, you will arrive at one of the six train stations in the capital (Lyon, Montparnasse, Est, Nord, Austerlitz, Saint-Lazare), or at one of the three stations in the Ile de France region (Massy TGV, Marne-la-Vallée-Chessy, Aéroport Charles-de-Gaulle TGV). Don't forget to reserve in advance, particularly if you're taking a TGV, or if you're leaving on a busy day, especially on weekends. Certain discounts are available for families with children, senior citizens, married couples and students. A "Joker" ticket offers reductions, but it must be purchased up to 30 days in advance.

Before boarding your train, don't forget to punch (*composter*) your ticket in one of the orange *composteur* machines.

All of the Paris train stations have excellent bus and métro connections. On arrival, a train, bus, métro or taxi

SNCF INFORMATION

Direct line:
☎ 08.36.35.35.35
(2.23 FF/min).
Information and sales Grandes Lignes (from 7am to 10pm).
Recorded message:
☎ 08.36.67.68.69
(1.49 FF/min).
Schedules for the Grandes Lignes (24 hours a day).
Minitel:
3615 and 3616 SNCF
(1.29 FF/min).
Information and sales for the Grandes Lignes.
Internet:
www.sncf.fr.
Information on schedules and prices.

CURRENCY

The French franc is, of course, the currency used in all the shops, hotels, restaurants and museums. Traveller's cheques are accepted in the larger hotels and department stores, but restaurants and shops will often ask you to change them at bank first. There are no restrictions on the amount of curency you may bring into France.

(see p. 29) will take you to your hotel.

BY VOITURE

Since the 16th century, with the creation of a centralised government, Paris has been at the heart

d'informations routières (☎ 08 36 68 20 00). Once in the city, it's up to you to decide whether it's worth driving; you may be better off leaving your car at the hotel or in a public parking garage.

BY COACH
Many coaches arrive at the Gare Routière at the Porte de la Villette in northeastern Paris The main coach operator is *Eurolines* ☎ 01.49.72.51.51.

TAX-FREE GOODS

Tourists (older than 15) living outside the European Community can reclaim the VAT (sales tax) provided they spend more than 2,000 francs in the same store. You must pay the tax; with the *détaxe* receipt, you are reimbursed after leaving the country.

of the national road and, starting in the 19th century, rail system. In France, all roads do indeed lead to Paris. The major autoroutes arrive the *périphérique,* or ring road. Check your final destination and choose the Porte (the main roads leading into Paris) accordingly. Be prepared for heavy traffic.
You can get information about traffic and road conditions by calling the Centre

CUSTOMS

POLICE
There are no visa requirements for European Community nationals (who need an identity card only) or for tourists from the United States and Canada (who must show a valid passport). For other countries, a visa may be necessary. Visitors planning a trip to France are advised to contact the French consulate in their country before leaving. If you bring along your chihuahua or tom cat, take a vaccination certificate signed by a veterinary.

SCENIC PARIS

"All the world's a stage," especially Paris! It's an international showcase for history and the arts. Feast your eyes on its palaces, monuments and churches, which reflect a time when artistic patronage and religious conviction created wonders. The museums house magnificent collections, and there is no lack of places to view paintings, antiques, fashion and design. Even the shop windows are created by the best contemporary decorators. Paris is, indeed, an eternal pageant.

THE SEINE SCENE

The Seine is both the heart and mirror of Paris. A river trip will take you back in time. Visiting Notre Dame and the surrounding streets is like being in the Middle Ages; Île Saint-Louis and the Marais area are steeped in 17th-century history. The Louvre was once the setting for royal splendour, and the Conciergerie witnessed the last days of the royal family. The Concorde is a prime example of sophisticated 18th-century architecture. The Grand Palais and the Petit Palais are lavish in style, especially compared to the more sober Invalides; and the Palais de Chaillot was built for the last Universal Exhibition.

THE INTERNATIONAL SCENE

Paris is a world unto its own, a maker and breaker of fashions, yet it is also open to influences from all over the world. It is probably the only city in France where you can step through a doorway and find yourself in a foreign land: the Russian community has its churches, conservatory, grocery stores and restaurants. The Rue du Faubourg Saint-Denis is the domain of Pakistanis and Sri Lankans. The famous Rue des Rosiers is the traditional heart of the Jewish quarter. The shops in Barbès and La Chapelle have the atmosphere of a souk; and you can step right out of the West and into Asia by visiting the Avenue de Choisy or Belleville, where the Vietnamese stores display exotic fruits on the sidewalk.

SETTING THE STAGE

The interior design of many galleries, boutiques, cafés and restaurants are the work of the most fashionable Parisian designers. Elegance and refinement have stepped into the world of marketing: Andrée Putman designed the *Et Vous* stores in the Rue Royale; the Italian designer Citterio did the *Esprit* store on the Place des Victoires; Willmotte was the

creator of *Junko Koshino*;
Garouste and Bonetti designed
rooms for the couturier
Christian Lacroix;
Jean-Paul Gaultier dreamt up
the Gaultier gallery in the
Faubourg Saint-Antoine;
Olivier Gagnère decorated
the *Bernardaud* tea room;
and Elizabeth de Portzamparc
designed the café at the
Cité de la Musique.

BEHIND THE SCENES

Paris is full of hidden
treasures; push open a door
and you can discover a
delightful courtyard, where

100-year-old trees
shade lovely old
buildings. Shops
now occupy these
enchanting
courtyards. Visit
the *Étoile d'or,* the
18th-century working-class
houses on the Faubourg Saint-
Antoine (n° 75) or the *Arbre à
Lettres* bookstore (n° 62).
Or the glass-roofed Casal
fabrics store in the Rue des
Saints-Pères (n° 40).
The workshops at 21,
Avenue du

Maine are worth a visit (the
Lieu-Dit florist, and the
decorator William Foucault).
Visit the Mohanjeet gallery
in the Rue Jacob (Cour de
Saxe) and the Triff gallery
(n° 12 and 35). In the Rue de
Seine, don't miss *Au Fond de
la Cour* at n° 49; or *Marion
Held Javal* at 5, Rue des
Petits-Champs. *Vivement
Jeudi,* 52, Rue Mouffetard,
is another picturesque place
to visit.

THE ITALIAN SCENE

There is a hint of Italy
on every Parisian street
corner. Armani is on the
Place Vendôme near the
Ritz, and is soon to open
a new store on the Place
Saint-Germain-des-Prés,
where the Drugstore Publicis
used to be. Prada, Sergio Rossi,
Fausto Santini, Angelo
Tarlazzi and Max Mara
all show their collections
from the Rue de
Grenelle to the Rue

du Cherche-Midi. Gianfranco
Ferre is on Avenue Georges-V,
and Versace is on the
Faubourg Saint-Honoré, near
Hermès. There are also plenty
of Italian grocers, caterers and
restaurants.

DEYROLLE BOUTIQUE

Deyrolle (46, Rue du Bac,
métro Rue du Bac)
is a strange and timeless
place, and has been a
favourite with nature-lovers
for the last two centuries.
It is a veritable treasure-
trove, with a collection
of stuffed animals, insects
and minerals that is unique
in Europe. Admire the lions,
crocodiles and snakes,
all frozen in time,
then stop to appreciate
the bright colours of
a butterfly from Ecuador,
or the beauty of a shell
from the Pacific.

PARIS ARCADES

Arcades are a Parisian invention. They thread their way between houses, or form secret passageways from one street to another. They became fashionable during the Restoration and the July Monarchy, aided by real-estate speculation, and were popular meeting places, to see and be seen. Nowadays, even if the crowds have gone, they are still full of the kind of charm and mystery which appeals to the Parisian soul.

IN THE BEGINNING

In 1785, the duke of Orléans was in need of money and decided to sell the arcades he had constructed in his garden at the Palais-Royal. He linked the Galerie de Montpensier to the Galerie de Valois with a wooden bridge, on which a variety of merchants soon set up shop. The arcade was born, and it became an instant success. Indeed, after the Revolution, speculators copied the idea, buying up the land that had become available through the sales of state property to build more arcades.

THE GOOD TIMES

The Vivienne, Colbert and Véro-Dodat Galleries opened in 1826. Glass roofs replaced the simple skylights which had first studded the ceilings; the wooden posts were removed to make the windows

larger; and cast-iron made the structure more solid. From 1817, the arcades were lit by gas lights. People flocked to the restaurants and cafés, the book stores and reading-rooms, the cake-shops and candy stores. Milliners and dressmakers also set up shop. The bourgeoisie, dazzled by such newly accessible luxury, spent lavishly and came to dance at the evening balls.

THE DECLINE. . .

When Louis-Philippe was on the throne, he put an end to

the prostitution and gambling which were rife in the gardens of the Palais-Royal. This was the coup de grace for the other arcades too. Under Napoleon III, the capital was increasingly urbanised and modernised.

Spectacular new buildings were constructed, and Parisians gradually turned their attention away from their previous centres of interest; what had once inspired their enthusiasm had become outmoded. In the 1878 Baedeker guide, the Parisian arcades were not even mentioned.

BACK IN FASHION

The arcades have now been renovated, and are visited once

couturiers, journalists, advertising people and their entourages now use the arcades as meeting places, thus reviving a tradition which appeared to have died out.

WHERE TO GO

For fashion, decoration and books: Galerie Vivienne (see p. 41). Passage Choiseul is an interesting mix of clothes and toy shops, poster shops, telephone boutiques and so on. Visit the stylish Galerie Véro-Dodat (see p. 40) for secondhand or antique dealers, leather goods and publishers.

The Passage des Panoramas (between the Rue Saint-Marc and Boulevard Montmartre) is worth a visit and is a good place for a lunch or coffee break. In Passage Jouffroy, there are interesting things to see at Thomas Boog, and Pain d'Épices is a charming store.

You will also enjoy a stroll down Passage Verdeau, especially if you are keen on drawings, engravings, old books and postcards.

. . . AND FALL

The years passed. By the early 1960s, the Galerie Colbert was being used as a warehouse, and its rotunda, a parking lot! When the glass roof of the Galerie Vivienne collapsed under the weight of the workman who was repairing it, nobody seemed to care. But then, during the 1980s, fashion houses moved into the Place des Victoires and its nearby area, and fabric designers into the Rue du Mail and the Rue des Petits-Champs. Parisians rediscovered the charm of the covered arcades in the neighbourhood of Paris, which had been practically forgotten since the last century.

more. The little shops Balzac described in *Les Illusions Perdues* have been replaced by decorators and fashion boutiques, which have moved in next to the surviving booksellers, secondhand dealers and craftshops. Existing cafés are frequented again, and new ones have opened. The world of designers,

PARIS IN BLOOM

April in Paris is not the only time to enjoy its flowers and fragrances, from the most humble to the most exotic. You could even do a "floral tour" of the city, which would wind its way from florist to florist, taking you through markets and public gardens and along the tree-lined avenues. It would be a new way to visit the capital, which all year round, presents a constantly changing pageant of colours.

Élysées was transformed into an enormous field of wheat, thereby bringing a symbol of France's agricultural wealth right into the heart of its capital.

TOWN AND COUNTRY

As early as the 17th century, the elegant buildings in the Marais had beautiful gardens. Marie de Médicis' Luxembourg Gardens, which were a favourite of 18th-century writers and artists, have hardly changed since Chalgrin completed them in the early 1800s. The present layout of the Tuileries is now similar to Le Nôtre's original design; and when Paris celebrated the bicentennial of the Revolution, the Champs-

THE PERFECT SITE

Paris is well qualified to be a "flower capital" for several reasons: it is a wealthy city, with a tradition of good taste and a certain nostalgia for the countryside. It is also situated in the heart of a horticultural region. Even its sprawling suburban development has not destroyed this tradition. The names of southern suburbs, such as Belle Épine, l'Hay-les-Roses and Fontenay-aux-Roses, remind us that this is still the rose-growing centre of the country. The Vexin area provides the bulbs which beautify the capital all year round; and

masses of flowers arrive daily from southern France to the Paris airports, just 30 minutes outside the city.

PUBLIC GARDENS

The City of Paris gardeners tend lovingly to the upkeep of the flower beds and borders which adorn the 400 or so public gardens and city avenues. The flowered walks

change with the seasons in the Luxembourg Gardens, and the Champs-Élysées has fine floral displays all year round, which tourists love to photograph. The Bagatelle park is famous for its roses and 100-year-old trees; and the Jardin des Plantes boasts a huge variety of species. The floral park at Vincennes must be seen when its valley is carpeted with stocks, tulips, pansies, and a quite exceptional collection of irises. Nearly 100,000 plants are grown every year in the magnificent Auteuil greenhouses, which were constructed during Napoleon III's reign.

GREEN POLITICS

The City of Paris administers some 7,600 acres of parks and gardens, and an impressive 600,000 trees, which makes one tree per 3.5 Parisians! Every year, the municipal gardeners plant 3,100 new trees, 215,000 perennials and climbing plants, and 3,000,000 green or flowering plants! Whenever they can save a green space or add a touch of

greenery to the urban environment, landscape architects try to instil a little extra chlorophyll into the city's atmosphere. New parks include Les Halles, the André Citroën park, the Belleville garden, the park at La Villette and the Arsenal pleasure-port, plus the latest acquisition, the promenade along the Daumesnil viaduct, called the "green trail", which goes from Bastille to the Vincennes park.

BOUQUETS AND BLOOMS

Plants and flowers seem to correspond to a need in the 1990s for a natural antidote to the noise, stress and pollution of the city. Apart from the specialist markets, here are some of the best addresses if you're looking for a beautiful bouquet:

■ **Christian Tortu**
6, Carrefour de l'Odéon, 75006, ☎ 01.43.26.02.56

■ **Marianne Robic**
41, Rue de Bourgogne, 75007, ☎ 01.44.18.03.47
■ **Michel Léger**
69, Rue de Grenelle, 75007, ☎ 01.45.49.09.70
■ **Liliane François**
64, Rue de Longchamp, 75016, ☎ 01.47.27.51.52
■ **Baptiste**
23, Rue des Saints-Pères, 75006, ☎ 01.42.60.11.90
■ **Lambert-Bayard**
6, Rue du Renard, 75004, ☎ 01.42.72.17.40

The refined and sophisticated bouquets are another of the aesthetic pleasures which Paris has to offer.

MONCEAU FLEURS

84, Blvd Raspail, 75006. ☎ 01.45.48.70.10. M° Saint Placide or Rennes. Mon.-Sat. 9am-8pm, Sun. 9am-1:30pm. And also: 11, Blvd Henri IV 75004; 92, Blvd Malesherbes 75008; 60, Ave. Paul Doumer 75016; 2, Pl. du Gal Koening, 75017; 94, Blvd des Invalides 75007

This is the chain of florists that Parisians prefer. The choice is huge, the flowers always fresh and the prices unbeatable. You can often find beautiful roses from 5 francs each, and 100 francs will buy you a magnificent bouquet.

INTELLECTUAL PARIS

"France is the oven in which humanity's intellectual bread is baked," or so said the Cardinal Eudes de Châteauroux in the 13th century. Paris became the country's capital in 987 with the coronation of Hugues Capet, and its reputation as a city of ideas, of philosophical trends, of literary and artistic creativity, and of protest movements, has always reached far beyond its frontiers. France's publishers, bookshops, press groups and media companies opt to be in Paris. The intelligentsia still gather at Parisian dinner parties, and cafés and restaurants fondly remember the golden age when they were frequented by the likes of Sartre, Cocteau or Fitzgerald.

THE PROLOGUE

In the Middle Ages, the finest minds were attracted to the capital. People came from the provinces or abroad to study in Paris, and many colleges grew up around the Sorbonne, which opened in 1257. The Latin Quarter (so-called because teaching was done in Latin) became the centre of all intellectual activity. Its reputation grew with the founding of the Collège de France in 1530; these universities then attracted the publishing industry.

BRANCHING OUT

The intellectual influence of Paris continued to spread. The French kings acquired an entourage of intellectuals, scientists and artists. French philosophers exported their ideas during the 18th century; Voltaire and Rousseau were known throughout Europe, foreign courts modelled themselves on Versailles, and Parisian salons were famous

for their wit and humour. The 19th century saw the genius of writers like Balzac, Zola, Flaubert and Eugène Sue. And the early 20th century is captured forever in the pages of Proust.

BOOKSELLERS

The Parisian bookshops or *bouquinistes* played an important role in the circulation of books. In 1857, there were 68; a certain Laîné

is known to have handled nearly 150,000 volumes every year. Bookstores such as we know them today did not yet exist, but there were "reading rooms" and "literary salons", which were often part of publishing houses. Books could be borrowed there for a fee, and intellectuals met to read the latest publications or to settle into a comfortable armchair and devour the foreign press—much like Stendhal, who used to frequent the Galignani book store.

SOMETHING FOR EVERYONE

One of the advantages of being in Paris is that you can find whatever books you're looking for. Theatre fans spend hours at the *Librairie Théatrale* (3, Rue Marivaux, 75002, 01.42.96.89.42) or at the

WRITERS IN PARIS

The streets of the Left Bank are full of memories. Balzac took up printing and publishing at 17, Rue Visconti, before starting to write. Racine spent the last years of his life at n° 24 of the same street. Delacroix painted at the Place de Furstenberg. L'Hôtel, in the Rue des Beaux-Arts, will always be linked to Oscar Wilde. Abbot Prévost, author of *Manon Lescaut*, lived at 12, Rue Saint-Séverin; Alphonse Daudet and Charles Cros at 7, Rue de Tournon. Pascal wrote his Pensées at 54, Rue Monsieur-le-Prince; Sainte-Beuve lived in the Cour du Commerce Saint-André, and Verlaine in the Rue de la Harpe.

Entrée des Artistes (161, Rue Saint-Martin, 75003, 01.48.87.78.58), where they are greeted on arrival by an extraordinary collection of automata. Globetrotters (or would-be globetrotters) can dream at the *Astrolabe* (14, Rue Serpente, 75006, 01.46.33.80.06) or at Ulysse (26, Rue Saint-Louis-en-l'Ile, 75004, 01.43.25.17.35). The *Librairie Gourmande* (4, Rue Dante, 75005, 01.43.54.37.27) is a great place for gourmets to devour books. And botanists find it hard to resist the *Maison Rustique* (26, Rue Jacob, 75006, 01.43.25.67.00).

THE LEFT BANK

When Abélard (1079-1142, considered to be the first French philosopher) was ousted by the canons of Notre-Dame, he crossed the Seine with his students and began to teach on the Left Bank. The Latin Quarter was born. Nowadays, despite the proliferation of universities and faculties in the outskirts of Paris, the fifth and sixth *arrondissements* are still a centre for students, with plenty of their favourite cafés, alternative cinemas, and university book stores. Any self-respecting member of the Parisian intelligentsia lives there too.

CAFÉ-SOCIETY

Paris wouldn't be Paris without its cafés. From Trocadéro to Saint-Germain, from Montparnasse to the Bastille, they harbour and record all the agitation of the capital. Many a new idea has taken shape around a bottle of wine, many of the world's problems have been solved at the bar, many a secret has been whispered across a pedestal table. Voltaire and Rousseau were regulars at the *Procope,* in the Rue des Fossés-Saint-Germain, in the 18th century.

CAFÉS AND POLITICS

The café soon became the ideal place for debating fashionable ideas. Diderot and d'Alembert are said to have launched the *Encyclopédie* in

the *Procope.* Camille Desmoulins frequented the cafés at Palais-Royal. In the 19th century, *Tortoni* was a popular meeting place for the intelligentsia of the grand boulevards; and in later days, Trotsky was to be found at the *Closerie des Lilas.* The *Café de Flore* was famous for its existentialist clientele, notably Jean-Paul Sartre and Simone de Beauvoir.

THE FIRST CAFÉ

Not until 1684 did Paris have its first café, the *Procope,* and it was a Sicilian, Signor Procopio, who opened it. It was an instant success, especially as the Comédie Française set up on the other side of the street, and Parisian theatre-goers began to stop at the café, appreciating the taste of the new beverage imported from the East. Racine is said to have written his plays with a cup of coffee in his hand.

meters, as decreed by the City of Paris). The Americans who discovered Paris after World War II were delighted by these impromptu terraces. They are featured in many films from the 1950s, including *An American in Paris* and *Funny Face.* Parisian terraces, whether those of fashionable cafés or traditional bistros, have a charm all of their own. They are places to see and to be seen; places to be actor or spectator, according to your style and your mood. The ultimate in chic at the moment is to carry on an important telephone conversation on your portable phone, while your captive lunch companions wait!

A BIT OF HISTORY

Towards the end of the Russian retreat in March of 1814, the Cossacks pursued Napoleon's armies into Paris, which was then occupied by Russians, Prussians and Austrians. The French word *bistrot* originates fom this period. When they wanted to have a quick drink, the Cossacks went into inns and taverns shouting "bistro, bistro...", which means "quick" in Russian. Today, Paris bistros tend to be small, moderately-priced restaurants with a limited, but often very good, selection of food.

Café de Flore, as did André Breton, Albert Camus and others. Their conversations and observations in such surroundings often gave birth to a new novel or play.

PARISIAN TERRACES

When the sun shines, the tables come out of the cafés onto the sidewalks, leaving just enough room for pedestrians (entitled to a width of 1.40 to 1.60

ARTISTS' CAFÉS

The cafés in Montparnasse and Saint-Germain-des-Prés were regular watering holes for writers and painters. Apollinaire went from one café to another, one neighbourhood to another; Modigliani paid his debts at *La Rotonde* with 14 paintings, which were burnt when he died. Truman Capote and Ernest Hemingway had their tables at the *Closerie des Lilas.* They also went to the

WAITER!

In certain establishments through the late 1930s, it was customary for Parisian café waiters to buy their own aprons. The traditional outfit is a black bow tie, a vest with pockets, a long white apron reaching down to the shoes, or a white jacket and black trousers.

A waiter can walk 10 to 20 kilometres a day on his rounds from one table to another. He is often the customer's confidante, the one who knows or guesses all kinds of secrets, but reveals nothing. Every year, the City of Paris and the Syndicate of Café-Owners organise a "waiters' and waitresses' race", when the public can admire their speed and skill as they carry a trayful of drinks through the streets of the capital.

A GOURMET'S PARIS

Paris is a rich country where agriculture, farming and fishing are of prime importance, and it's hardly surprising that the city should be a gourmet's paradise. Kings employed the best chefs; master pastry-makers invented the delicious cakes we still enjoy today. There are many references in literature to abundant markets, culinary extravaganzas, passing food-fads. The shop windows are a constant temptation, with sweet and savoury delights. Go on in, give yourself a treat and get a taste of Paris!

to relish foreign flavours. Hédiard started the trend in 1860, with the "Spices and Colonies Counter" in the Rue Notre-Dame-de-Lorette, which sold unfamiliar spices and exotic fruits and vegetables. In 1886, Auguste

Fauchon set up his fruit and vegetable stall at the Place de la Madeleine, and Parisians flocked to taste his regional produce. The rest is history.

Les Halles, or marketplace, of Paris in the 19th century.

THE BELLY OF PARIS

In 1855, at the request of Napoleon III, the architect Baltard designed the huge iron construction known as "Les Halles". This central food market became an important feature of the city. The late-night customers in the nearby restaurants and bars would mingle in the early hours with the strong-armed market-workers. In 1969, when the Halles moved out to Rungis on the outskirts of the city, something of the soul of Paris went with them. Today, the market covers 232 hectares, and some 28,000 vehicles leave daily with food supplies to feed one-fifth of the population of France.

DELICATESSENS

A new kind of grocery opened its doors in the 19th century, and Parisian taste-buds began

A SWEET TRADITION

In the 16th century, the pastry-maker would sing his wares in the streets, to draw in some customers. In 17th-century

Paris, Ragueneau invented the "amandine", a delicious almond tart, and Vatel concocted Chantilly cream. In the 1800s, Carême first made nougat and meringues. The fondant made its appearance in 1830, followed by candied chestnuts in 1835. During the same period, the Sergent cake-shop in the Rue du Bac was famous for its "millefeuille"; and a certain Quillet made the first butter cream in 1865.

FOR THE LOVE OF CHOCOLATE

Anne of Austria first brought chocolate to Paris via Spain and the conquistadors.

The first manufacturer of chocolate liqueurs and pastilles opened its doors in 1659. It was the ultimate in chic, and the Marquise de Sévigné mentioned it in her letters. Nowadays, Paris boasts many exceptional chocolate-makers: Robert Linxe, Christian Constant, Pierre Hermé for Fauchon, Dalloyau, Lenôtre, Debauve and Gallais. On winter afternoons, Parisians and tourists alike queue to taste the rich and creamy hot-chocolate drink served in the famous *Angélina* tea room. Paris even has a Chocolate-Crunchers' Club for chocaholics!

A TASTE FOR THE EXOTIC

Paris is the only city in France where it's easy to find food from all over the world. Africa and the West Indies, Asia and the Mediterranean, America and Russia, the Near East and Scandinavia. There are more and more specialist food stores, catering to the widest variety of tastes and bringing the best of foreign traditions to the pleasure-seeking Parisians.

Fruits, vegetables, spices, condiments, charcuterie and candies. You have the whole world in your plate!

LET THEM EAT CAKE

Even though it's served in cafés at breakfast time with coffee, the famous croissant is far from Parisian in origin. It is, in fact, one of the appropriately named "Viennoiseries", imported from Austria. As for the brioche, it was invented in 1690 in Paris, as was the baguette (weighing 250 gr) which first appeared in the 1960s. The larger *pain*, which weighs 400 gr, is also Parisian in origin; it is made of white flour and is kneaded in a special way.

TREASURE-HUNTER'S PARIS

On Saturday mornings, Paris is for treasure-hunters. Shake yourself awake, and head off to the flea markets. You'll find a vast array of furniture and objects piled on shelves, spilling onto the sidewalks and filling up the alleyways. The search is on, and who knows, you may even find your heart's delight.

A SHORT STORY ABOUT A GREAT FLEA MARKET

It all started with the rag merchants who set up in the late 19th century outside the city walls, to avoid paying the toll that was levied inside the city. They chose Saint-Ouen because the inhabitants of Montmartre hill passed through there on their way down to the dance halls. A certain bourgeoisie, always on the lookout for excitement, came here to rough it with the café and dance hall crowds, and on their way they stopped to look at the extraordinary piles of rags and bric-a-brac. They soon took more than just a passing interest and began to buy. Thus a new fashion was started, and in 1891 the flea market was born. It has continued to grow ever since.

FLEA MARKET STYLE

Appearances can be deceptive! Don't be fooled by the stallholder who's playing cards or sharing a picnic with his mates, at a stall that seems to be full of junk. He may well be an aristocrat in disguise, who relishes the flea market with its unique atmosphere, and the freedom it gives him. Don't suppose, either, that you'll find the most fantastic bargains; you're dealing with a professional who knows his stuff and knows what it's worth! Dress casually to go to the flea markets; cultivate a relaxed and indifferent air, and never let on what you're looking for!

MARCHE BIRON

SAINT-OUEN FLEA MARKET: WHAT'S WHAT

Everyone goes to Saint-Ouen. All walks of life rub shoulders at the countless stalls of the ten separate markets (not counting the "Usine", which is for professionals only), covering nearly 76 acres. It's the world's largest antiques market! It's not worth getting up at the crack of dawn to come here, as most stalls open about 9 or 9.30am on Saturdays, Sundays and Mondays, and close at 6pm. The markets all have a different flavour: Vernaison has something of everything, from jewellery to lights, while Biron is more expensive, with furniture for wholesalers from New York's East Side. At the Serpette market, certain stallholders tend to specialise in 1930s objects. Paul Bert is still the most authentic "flea market", where you can look around and hunt through the things yourself, and indeed, many designers and decorators come here. For leather jackets, jeans, Doc Martens, and sometimes pickpockets too, go to the Malik market. And when you're ready to drop and starving for lunch, take a break in one of the many cafés or restaurants, avoiding the lunch-time rush hour if you possibly can. (For other flea markets, see p. 112.)

WHAT TO BUY, HOW TO PAY

There's no point in offering 10,000 francs for a table if the asking price is 20,000 francs. It's better to compare prices, and consider how much an object is worth before you start haggling. You often get better results by chatting with the stallholder and establishing a friendly contact; it also helps if you pay cash. Don't hesitate to go away and come back ten minutes later; the object won't disappear, and even if it does, so what! They will hold it for you, or let you pay on an instalment plan. If it's expensive, you should ask for a dated and detailed invoice, which facilitates things if you resell it or it is stolen (for the insurance forms).

padlocked to protect the treasures inside: old books, papers, engravings, postcards and posters. The collections are of mixed interest and quality; but if you take the time to look, ignoring the noise and pollution from the passing cars, you just may chance upon that special something.

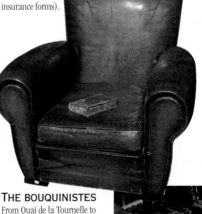

THE BOUQUINISTES

From Quai de la Tournelle to Quai Voltaire on the Left Bank, and from Quai de l'Hôtel-de-Ville to Quai du Louvre on the Right, the secondhand bookshops, or *bouquinistes*, are all part of the special charm of Paris. They've been there as long as the Pont-Neuf, constructed by Henri IV. Their lacquered green wooden boxes are secured to the parapets and

PARIS FASHION

Only in Paris do some 2,000 journalists and 800 buyers gather together when the haute-couture and ready-to-wear collections go on show. Karl Lagerfeld may be German; John Galliano, British; and Gianfranco Ferre, Italian, but Paris is still the fashion capital of the world. Asians and Americans arrive twice a year, to be the first to see the new designs which will be worn from the Pacific to the Atlantic. Parisian chic is still in a class of its own.

Christian Lacroix haute Couture hiver 97

FASHION SHOWS

The ritual fashion shows, at which couturiers from all over the world present the results of months of work, are now held at the Carrousel du Louvre. It's the same every year: people crowd at the door, rush to their seats, look around to see who's there, and then wait. The atmosphere is electric, while behind the scenes the tension grows. Then on come the spotlights, the music starts, and the world's top models step out onto the catwalk. The shows are wonderful publicity for the spin-off industries of accessories, perfumes and cosmetics.

THE BUYERS

After the last war, there were still 20,000 women who wore haute couture. Now there are only 200 throughout the world. Almost 80 per cent of the clientele is foreign: American first, then Asian and European. Arab princesses used to be prime customers, but they have been much more discreet since the Gulf War. A couturier dress requires at least 100 hours of extremely painstaking work, and three or four trying-on sessions; it costs more than 50,000 francs, while an evening dress is priced at four times as much. This is why haute-couture only accounts for 6 per cent of couturiers' real turnover. However, these prestigious creations are still fantastic publicity for the fashion houses' less exclusive productions.

DESIGN AND MARKETING

To keep in tune with changes in society and in the economic situation, fashion designers and couturiers tend to develop a wide range of accessories and ready-to-wear. This trend began back in the 1970s, a period when teenagers really began to count in the marketplace, both as consumers (even if their buying power was relatively limited) and fashion-makers in their own right. New names came to the fore, and designers became attentive to the needs of this new clientele. Kenzo, Agnès B., Dorothée Bis, Emanuelle Khanh, as well as Yamamoto and Comme des Garçons set up in Paris. Young people began to adopt an informal style which soon

became the norm in universities and trendy cafés; country-style shirts and jeans, the fashion statement.

1997, 68,000 faked articles were seized, but Italy continues to break production records and Indonesia, Thailand and the Philippines still flood the market with fakes, which means that French companies spend a lot of money trying to protect their products.

FAKES

There is always a price to pay for fame, and for haute-couture, it means falling victim to copies made abroad. Some people will go to any lengths to wear a famous name. Imitations are to be found at a fraction of the price, but the mediocre quality ultimately harms the image of the original, and the many copies are damaging both for the economy and for the export trade. The customs authorities and the police keep a sharp lookout; in

LUXURIOUS PARIS

During the last century, Guerlain perfumed the shoulders of many beautiful women. Eugénie de Montijo wore Worth dresses, and during the Roaring Twenties, many fashionable Parisians were dressed by Poiret. The names of Dior, Hermès, Cartier, Puiforcat and Lalique conjure up a certain inimitable, quintessentially Parisian idea of luxury. Nowadays, that luxury has become more accessible, but the charm and seduction remain intact.

Mademoiselle Chanel in 1935

(a body which groups luxury trades together) makes interesting reading, especially for the dates when certain companies were founded: Révillon, 1723; Baccarat, 1764; Château d'Yquem, 1786;

Puiforcat, 1820; Hermès, 1837; Boucheron, 1858; Bernardaud, 1863; Lanvin, 1889; Lalique, 1910. Luxury tends to last, and is to be found in many trades, from fashion to silverware, from jewellery to perfume, from decoration to crystalware.

THE PRICE OF LUXURY

Certain names still have the power to make people dream, and some dreams only come true if you can afford to pay for them. The price of luxury is relative, however. It's a question of authenticity, of the best materials, of exclusiveness, of respect for the craftsman's skill. Christian Dior used to say that no price is too high to pay for absolute quality. The famous *Kelly* bag by Hermès requires 18 hours of work and uses the finest quality leathers; it costs about 14,000 francs, but lasts a lifetime. A pure crystal Baccarat glass, handmade by a master craftsman, costs about 400 francs, but it's a genuine collector's item.

THE CAPITAL OF LUXURY

In France, luxury is often associated with authentic regional produce, but although silk comes from Lyon, perfumes from around Paris, silverware from Normandy and porcelain from Limoges, Paris is still the showcase, where it all happens, where everything is created and everything is sold, often to a foreign clientele. The brochure produced by the Comité Colbert

WHO OWNS IT?

Most luxury firms are still French-owned, saved by buyouts or restructuring. The Puiforcat silversmiths

Parisian luxury need not be viewed from a distance. You can push open the door of a great fashion house and step right into a dream world of elegance and refinement. At Dior, you can walk around as you please, from one showcase to the next; the well-trained sales staff are discreet, and you needn't be intimidated by their uniform (blue or black, depending on the address). Don't be afraid to look around at Hermès either; there's no obligation to buy. You'll see plenty of Japanese, who are not at all uncomfortable in such surroundings.

and the Saint-Louis crystal works now belong to Hermès. The Wertheimer family have owned Chanel since 1924, and the LVMH group own Christian Dior, Givenchy, Christian Lacroix, Vuitton, Moët & Chandon, Hennessy and Kenzo. Cardin owns his own brand name and its many licences; the Sanofi group has Yves Saint Laurent, Nina Ricci, and Roger & Gallet. As regards the top hotels, the situation is

rather different; the Crillon is still French, but the Ritz is Arab-owned, the Plaza and the George V are American and the Bristol is German.

WHO BUYS IT?

Apart from haute couture, luxury products have become more democratic and are more accessible now than they used to be. Licences, franchises and company policies have helped to diversify and multiply such products, and with the advent of advertising, famous names have became household words, giving the related products a wider popular appeal. Couturier ranges of accessories or ready-to-wear collections (with names like *Bis, Parallèle, Bazar* and *Diffusion*) are sold at competitive prices, but the style and quality are maintained. Silversmiths, porcelain manufacturers and crystal engravers always include less expensive items in their collections and constantly adapt them to suit changing tastes.

STREETS OF LUXURY

Each capital, from New York, Tokyo and London to Milan, has its own luxury district,

where prestigious stores tend to group together. Potential customers visit these areas and feast on the window displays. Streets such as Avenue Montaigne, Faubourg Saint-Honoré, Rue François-Ier, Rue Royale and Place Vendôme are synonymous with luxury. In recent years, Saint-Germain-des-Prés has also seen an influx of luxury stores. Armani, Lacroix, Vuitton and de Castelbajac have joined Yves Saint Laurent at the Place Saint-Sulpice, thereby recuperating a Left Bank clientele that sometimes prefers to leave the Right Bank to the tourists.

PARISIAN DEPARTMENT STORES

Paris can be compared to a huge department store. From the Middle Ages onwards, the various trade associations were grouped together in guilds, which set up shop in a particular district. This tradition still survives today, thereby imprinting a specific character on certain areas of the capital.

A SPECIALITY PER NEIGHBOURHOOD

Bicycles and cars gleam in the shop windows of the Avenue de la Grande-Armée, crystal and porcelain in those of the Rue de Paradis, while Saint-Germain-des-Prés and Odéon are better known for their bookshops and publishers. You will find furniture (sometimes rather

showy) in the Faubourg Saint-Antoine; and musical instruments and sheet music in the Rue de Rome. Avant-garde fashion designers are at the Place des Victoires, and the main jewellers are in the Rue de la Paix and the Place Vendôme. The neighbourhood around the Marché Saint-Pierre, near the Sacré-Coeur, is the domain of fabrics. Ready-to-wear is mostly made in the Sentier district, not far from the one-time headquarters of most of the national papers. You'll find everything you need for your motorbike near the Place de la Bastille; computer shops have moved into the Avenue Daumesnil, near the Gare de Lyon station.

GREAT STORES THAT STARTED SMALL

Visiting a Parisian department store is rather like visiting a monument, except that entrance is free! Most of them are over a hundred years old. *Au Bon Marché* was the first of its kind, founded in 1852 by Aristide Boucicaut, and later immortalised by Émile Zola in his novel *Au*

Bonheur des Dames.
Jules Jaluzot, an ex-employee of this store, founded *Le Printemps* on the Right Bank in 1865. *La Samaritaine* was started in 1870 by Ernest Cognacq, a street vendor who

sold ties on the Pont-Neuf. Nowadays it is the biggest department store in the capital. The "newest" of these stores is the *Galeries*

Lafayette, a one-time fancy goods shop founded by Alphonse Kahn and Théophile Bader in 1899.

THE SPECIALIST STORES

Even though they are generalist by definition, the Parisian department stores often have their individual strong points. The *Bazar de l'Hôtel de Ville (BHV)* is a Mecca for do-it-yourself enthusiasts. La Samaritaine is famous for its hardware and gardening departments and its working clothes. The Printemps has a "Boutique Blanche" which is very popular for wedding lists. Au Bon Marché is a very smart and classic store, with an excellent food hall which is much frequented by the inhabitants of the Left Bank. Galeries Lafayette is better-known for fashion (especially clothes, but also perfumes and accessories). The department stores need to keep their customers' loyalty and interest, so they often organise exhibitions around a theme (China, Vietnam, England), which are usually very good. The culture of a country is presented along with typical products, antique furniture, arts and crafts or traditional clothes. Whether or not you intend to buy, these events are always interesting.

THE ARCHITECTURE

Au Bon Marché was built by Gustave Eiffel, and recently renovated by Andrée Putman who designed the sober lines of the central escalator. Le Printemps is like an enormous ocean liner; it has a glass dome, dating from 1923, which is 53 feet high and 66 feet in diameter. Galeries Lafayette also has an extraordinary double dome, which creates beautiful effects when the sunlight shines through it. The various buildings of La Samaritaine make up a fascinating anthology of commercial architecture from 1900 to 1930. Shop n° 2, near the Seine, has the most beautiful Art Deco-style façade in the capital. It was built in 1928 by Frantz Jourdain and Henri Sauvage. In 1932, shop n° 3 (on the corner of the Rue de Rivoli and Rue Boucher) was reconstructed in prefabricated materials in barely six months,

during which time customers continued to shop inside it. The interior staircase was recently renovated by Andrée Putman.

ADDRESSES

■ AU BON MARCHÉ,
22, Rue de Sèvres, 75007.

■ PRINTEMPS,
64, Blvd Haussmann, 75009.

■ GALERIES LAFAYETTE,
40, Blvd Haussmann, 75009.

■ LA SAMARITAINE,
19, Rue de la Monnaie, 75001.

■ BHV,
52, Rue de Rivoli, 75004.

What to see: practical information

With more than 2,100,000 people living in 39 square miles, divided into 20 *arrondissements,* Paris is simply too large to visit in a single day.

GETTING AROUND THE CITY

BY MÉTRO

The underground system is the fastest and easiest way to get around Paris. The maps are clear and well-marked, and there is almost always a station within a few blocks of where you want to go. With 15 different lines and many transfer stations, the métro system covers Paris like an underground spiderweb.

The métro is open from 5:30am to 12:30am. A single ticket is valid for any destination within the city limits. A tickets costs 8 francs (it is more economical to purchase a *carnet* of 10 tickets for 48 francs), and can be purchased in the métro, in tobacco shops *(tabacs)* and at the tourist office.

Métro passes for one or three days (30 or 105 francs) are good for an unlimited number of trips. The 105-franc pass, known as the *Paris Visite* card, offers a 25 to 35 per cent discount at certain Paris monuments and museums. Children under the age of 4 travel free on the métro and bus, while children 4 to 10 pay half-price.

BY BUS

This is the best way to actually see the city, especially if you get stick in a Paris traffic jam! There are 58 bus lines, plus the PC *(petite ceinture,* or small beltway), which travels around the edge of Paris via the ringroad. Buses run from 6:30am to 8:30pm or 12:30am, depending on the lines. Unfortunately, many lines do not run on Sundays or holidays. A late-night bus system, called the *Noctambus,* includes 10 lines that run every hour between 1:30am and 5:30am. Use the same ticket for a bus as for the métro: a single ticket per trip, no matter how far you're going in Paris. Free maps are available at the underground ticket counters.

> ## OFFICES OF THE RATP
>
> **Place de la Madeleine**
>
> You can get all the information you need at this office.
> Or try calling the answering machine at:
> ☎ 08.36.68.77.14.

For a comfortable way to see Paris, take the *Balabus*. Operated by the RATP, it runs on Sundays, from April 11 to September 26, from 12:30pm to 8pm. The 50-minute trip takes you from the Gare de Lyon to the Grande Arche de la Défense, and drives past all the major monuments in the capital.

BY TAXI

Taxis can be hailed on the street or at one of the taxi stations marked with a large sign. The metre starts running with an initial fare of about 13 francs. The rates go up after 7pm and outside the city limits; there is also an extra charge for pickups at train stations and airport terminals (about 10 francs), and for luggage (5 francs per suitcase). Taxi-drivers generally expect cash and a 10 per cent tip. A taxi is free if the light on the top is lit up (it's occupied when just a small bulb is on). Taxis can refuse you if your group has more than three people or an animal. Paris has a number of radio-dispatched taxi companies:

Taxis Bleus, ☎ 01.49.36.10.10; G7, ☎ 01.47.39.47.39; Taxis 7000, ☎ 01.42.70.00.42.

BY CAR!

Driving in Paris is not exactly relaxing if you're not used to the traffic and don't know your way around. Not to mention the challenge of finding a parking spot. Traffic wardens, who once wore easy-to-spot light blue uniforms, now patrol the streets in discreet navy blue. And they are quick to write out tickets (from 75 to 220 francs

apiece!). Although some streets forbid parking altogether, most allow pay parking (purchase a ticket from one of the metres on the street; you can park from 1 to 2 hours). On some streets, you may not park on Saturday, Sunday or holidays.

Underground parking areas are fairly expensive. Consider yourself forewarned: cars do get impounded in Paris. If you come out of a museum or café and can't find your car, it may have been towed (call ☎ 01.55.76.20.80). One last tip: buy a good map before you leave or first thing when you arrive.

You can get gas 24 hours a day at: Mobil, 151, Rue de la Convention, 75015; ou Total, George-V parking lot, 75008.

BY BIKE

Two years ago, with the municipal elections coming up, the city government created a series of lanes and streets reserved for bicycles (the quays along the Seine, for example, are closed to traffic on Sundays during the summer months). Bicycles are a great way to see the city, but be careful: cars won't make it easy for you. Depending on the weather conditions, the pollution levels can be fairly high on certain days. Some cyclers in Paris choose to wear masks. Bike rentals:
Paris à vélo c'est sympa,
☎ 01.48.87.60.01.
Paris-Vélo,
☎ 01.43.37.59.22.

BY BUS

You can "do" Paris by bus in just a few hours.
Cityrama,
4, pl. des Pyramides, 75001,
☎ 01.44.55.60.00.
Paris-Vision,
214, rue de Rivoli, 75001,
☎ 01.42.60.31.25.

POST OFFICE, TELEPHONES

Stamps are available at post offices (closed Sunday and Saturday after 12pm) and at tobacco shops. Yellow mailboxes are easily found on the streets (last pickup is around 6pm, 7pm at the post offices and from 8 to 10pm at the main post office located on the Rue du Louvre). Outgoing mail can also be left at the reception desk of

your hotel. The main post office (52, Rue du Louvre, 75001, ☎ 01.40.28.20.00.) is open 24 hours a day if you need to make a phone call or send a telegram when the others offices are closed.

You can use one of the many public telephone booths located throughout Paris to check in with the kids at home (it will be less expensive than a hotel phone). You will need a "Telecarte", which can be purchased at a post office or tobacco shop.

MONEY

Foreign currency can be exchanged at banks (closed Sunday and usually Saturday) and currency exchange offices. Small exchange offices are often open on Sundays in popular tourist areas: for example, at 1, Rue Hautefeuille, 75006, ☎ 01.46.34.70.46 or Thomas Cook, 8, Pl. de l'Opéra, 75009, ☎ 01.47.42.46.52.

SITES AND MONUMENTS

Most museums and monuments are open from 10am to 8pm six days a week (except for certain holidays). Smaller museums may close

during lunch hours, so it's wise to call ahead. National museums are closed on Tuesday; city of Paris museums are closed on Monday.

A museum and monument pass is a good way to explore Paris; it is good for free entrance to 70 museums and monuments in Paris and the surrounding region. A one-day pass costs 70 francs, a three-day pass, 140 francs. You can purchase them at museums, monuments and at the tourist office. If you're short on time, **Paristoric,** a 45-minute big-screen shown is an excellent introduction to the history of Paris. Shows run every hour, from 9am to 6pm or 9pm. **Paristoric:** 11 bis Rue Scribe, 75009. ☎ 01.42.66.62.06.

You have to do everything at least once, including a "bateau-mouche" trip on the Seine. It's ideal in good weather or for a romantic candle-lit dinner for two,

PARIS: PRACTICAL INFORMATION

If you want to find out what's happening in Paris and when (movies, theatre, exhibits, restaurants, museums and so on), buy one of the two weekly guides: *L'Officiel des Spectacles* or *Pariscope*.

Paris Tourist Office, 127, Champs-Élysées, 75008, ☎ 01.49.52.53.54. The tourist office is open daily 9am to 8pm. You'll find an enormous amount of useful information, guides and maps. You can purchase métro and bus tickets, and make hotel reservations. There are branch offices in all the train stations, except Saint-Lazare.

in the company of the most beautiful monuments of Paris.

Vedettes du Pont-Neuf, Square du Vert-Galant, ☎ 01.46.33.98.38.

Bateaux du pont de l'Alma, Right Bank, ☎ 01.42.25.96.10.

Bateaux parisiens, at the base of the Eiffel Tower, ☎ 01.44.11.33.55.

The Eiffel Tower and Trocadéro,
from one Universal Exhibition to another

One of the best views of Paris is from Trocadéro, looking past the Eiffel Tower to the Champs de Mars and the École Militaire. This setting was created for the Universal Exhibitions of 1889 and 1937. In the summer, cafés set up tables outdoors, while skateboards and skaters whiz around the marble-lined terraces of the Chaillot Palace, boom-boxes and walkmans in hand.

Musée Guimet

PLACE D'IÉNA

Rue de Lübeck

R. Gaston de St-Paul

Wilson

Avenue du Président

Av. Albert de Mun

Av. R. Fresnel

Avenue

New York

❹ Musée d'Art moderne

PLACE DU TROCADÉRO

Palais de Chaillot

Av. Gustave V de Suède

Nations Unies

de

Seine

Av. Albert 1er de Monaco

Av. des PLACE DE VARSOVIE

PONT D'IÉNA

Branly

Quai

❶ Tour Eiffel

❶ The Eiffel Tower ★★★
Champ-de-Mars, 75007.
☎ 01.44.11.23.23.
11am-11pm; June-Sept.: 24 hours a day. Entrance fee.

This old iron lady, constructed to celebrate the centennial of the French Revolution, carries her nearly 110 years with amazing grace. With 6 million visitors come every year, it is one of the most-visited monuments in Paris. You can walk up or take the lift to the upper platforms. There are shops, restaurants, lookouts, and one of the best views of Paris from nearly 1,000 feet high. On a clear day, you can see 55 miles away from the top platform.

❷ The Chaillot Palace ★★★
1, Pl. du Trocadéro, 75016.

Constructed for the 1937 Universal Exhibition, Chaillot houses museums, theatres and restaurants.
Théâtre Chaillot,
☎ 01.47.27.81.15. Two rooms and two repertories, one classical, the other contemporary.

Musée de l'Homme,
☎ 44.05.72.72. 9:45am-5:15pm; closed Tues.
Entrance fee.
An overview of mankind through prehistory, ethnology and anthropology.
Musée de la Marine,
☎ 01.53.65.69.69.
10am-6pm; closed Tues.
Entrance fee.
The history of the French navy

through a series of models. A perfect place to visit with kids. Le Totem, ☎ 01.47.27.28.29. Daily noon-2pm. The restaurant in the Musée de l'Homme also has a great view of the Eiffel Tower and Trocadéro Gardens which extend on either side of a long pool decorated with sculptures and fountains. At night, the fountains and palace are lit up to create a magnificent sight.

❸ Guimet Museum ★★★
19, Ave. d'Iéna, 75016.
☎ 01.45.05.00.98.
9:45 am-6 pm; closed Tuesday. Entrance fee.

The museum of Asiatic arts is closed for renovation until late 1998, but some sculptures can still be seen in the galleries of the Buddhist Pantheon.

❹ The Museum of Modern Art of the City of Paris ★★★
11, Ave. du Président-Wilson, 75016.
☎ 01.40.70.11.10.
10am-5:30pm, to 6:45pm on Sat. and Sun; closed Mon. Entrance fee.

This is the place to find a number of works by Vuillard, Picasso, Modigliani, van Dogen and Bonnard, as well as Matisse's panels of *The Dance,* finally brought together. The museum has a shop, bookshop and cafeteria with outdoor seating in good weather.

❺ Carette ★★
4, Pl. du Trocadéro, 75016.
☎ 01.47.27.88.56.
8am-7 pm; closed Tues. and Aug.

A charming, old-fashioned decor with macaroons as famous as the lovely terrace. A place for Parisians to see and be seen, along with a few occasional tourists.

❼ STROLLING THROUGH THE 16TH ★★

Leave the Place du Trocadéro by the Rue Benjamin Franklin (near the right wing of the Chaillot Palace), and stroll toward Passy and Auteuil. Balzac wrote his last novels at 47 Rue Raynouard (open 10am-5:15pm, closed Monday; entrance fee). To your right is the Maison de Radio France. Continue along the Rue La Fontaine, which has lovely Art Nouveau bow windows and wrought-iron railings.

❻ The Cinémathèque ★★
7, Ave. Albert-de-Mun, 75116.
☎ 01.47.04.24.24 (schedule updated daily, Wed. to Sun. afternoon)

Some film enthusiasts never miss a week; others watch three movies a day. Some 40,000 films, many of which are masterpieces, are kept, restored and projected in this temple to cinema. If you're visiting Paris, this may be your chance to see a rare showing. The schedule is published each week in the *Pariscope* or the *Officiel des Spectacles*.

The Champs-Élysées,
the showcase of Paris

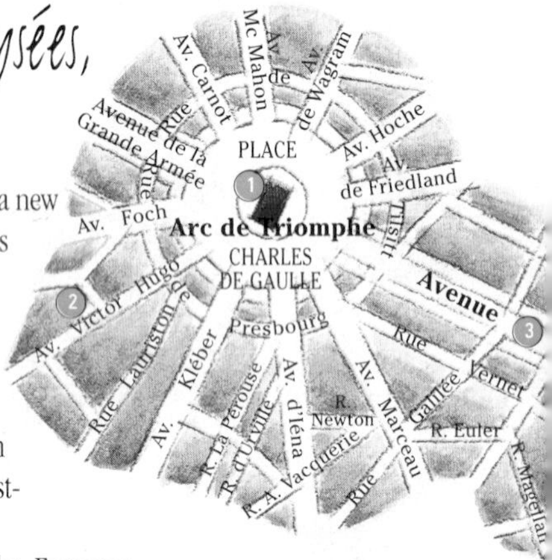

The Champs-Élysées has a new look: all the automobiles parked along the sidewalks are gone, and rows of trees have been planted in their place. Crowds pour out of every métro station on the weekend to fill up the fast-food restaurants, movie theatres and shopping arcades. For some unknown reason, Saturday mornings are different: the avenue is still calm, and the cafés offer a quiet haven to contemplate the majestic view.

(Map labels: Av. Mc Mahon, Av. de Wagram, Av. Carnot, Av. de Hoche, Avenue de la Grande Armée, Rue, PLACE, Av. Hoche, Av. de Friedland, Av. Foch, Arc de Triomphe, CHARLES DE GAULLE, Avenue, Av. Victor Hugo, Av. Kléber, Presbourg, Rue, Galilée Verner, Rue, Rue Lauriston, Av. La Pérouse, Av. d'Iéna, Av. d'Uckine, R. Newton, R. Galilée Marceau, R. Euler, R. A. Vacquerie, Rue)

An architectural jewel from the 1920s. The glass façade alone is worth the trip, as is the restaurant, which has a decor of black marble, mahogany, gold leaf and mosaics. This was one of the Windsors' favourite haunts when they were in Paris. Sit at the bar and order a seafood platter or oysters.

when morning light emphasizes the details of the sculpture. The view from the top is, of course, magnificent.

❷ Prunier Traktir ★★
16, Ave. Victor-Hugo, 75016.
☎ 01.44.17.35.85.
Mon. night-Sat. noon-11pm;
closed mid-June to mid-Aug.

❶ The Arc de Triomphe ★★★
Place du Général-de-Gaulle, 75008.
☎ 01.43.80.31.31. 9:30am-11pm; Sun., Mon.: 9:30am-6:30pm. Entrance fee.

Chalgrin drew up the plans for Napoleon I, who wanted a monument worthy of his great army. Yet fate decided otherwise. The work was not entirely completed until 1836, during the reign of Louis-Philippe. The best time to see the Arc is early in the day,

❸ The Champs-Élysées ★★★
In the late 17th century, the Champs Élysées was nothing more than an empty field

before Le Nôtre planted it with trees to extend the view past the Tuileries. During the Second Empire, a constant stream of horse-drawn carriages paraded up the street, so that women could show off their outfits. "The most beautiful street in the world" has lost

The Champs-Élysées at the turn of the century

much of its sparkle and prestige, but it is still a unique architectural ensemble.

❹ Fouquet's ★★

99, Ave. des Champs-Élysées, 75008.
☎ 01.47.23.70.60.
Daily 8am-2am.

Is there any famous figure who hasn't been here? The history of Fouquet's is tinged with nostalgia and elegance. The terrace on the corner of the Avenue George V is still one of the most beautiful in Paris. The speciality is the "César", the cocktail created by the bartender and dedicated to the famous French sculptor.

❺ Virgin Megastore ★

52, Ave. des Champs-Élysées, 75008.
☎ 01.49.53.50.00.
Mon. to Sat. 10am-midnight,
Sun. noon-midnight.

Virgin transformed a temple of money into a temple of music. The lovely marble architecture of the 1930s building, the former offices of the National City Bank of New York was left untouched. Several thousand people stop by every day to check out the multimedia, Internet, television, hi-fi, video, CD and cassette departments, as well as the bookshop and ticket outlet.

❻ Planet Hollywood ★

78, Ave. des Champs-Élysées, 75008.
☎ 01.53.83.78.27.
Daily 11am-1am.

The staircase is lined with plaster casts of Hollywood stars, while clothes and objects from mega-films made in America decorate the interior. The restaurant belongs to Sylvestor Stallone, Arnold Schwarzenegger and Bruce Willis, among others.

THE SHOPPING ARCADES ON THE CHAMPS-ÉLYSÉES

You can find everything from a teddy bear to Paris souvenirs and spangled jumpers in these arcades, yet the slick shops of the Galerie des Champs, Arcades du Lido, galerie Point-Show and galerie Élysées-La Boétie are rather expensive and filled with tourists.

The food is typical Tex-Mex or American fare. Kids love it, but it's crowded for lunch and dinner, and on Saturday nights.

Madeleine - Rue Saint-Honoré,
luxury and business

The neighbourhood around the fake Greek temple of the Madeleine awakens early with Japanese and American tourists shopping along the Rue Royale and the Faubourg Saint-Honoré, the showcase for French luxury goods with shops such as Hermès, Lalique and Christofle. Jewellery, crystal and porcelain boutiques line the streets of this neighborhood, along with the more recent interior design shops, where you can find furniture and the latest fabrics. Have a look around, even if you're not buying.

❶ Church of the Madeleine ★★★
7am-1:30pm and 3:30pm-7pm.

After many delays, it was the architect Vignon who finally designed the unique silhouette of this monument initially intended as a temple to Glory. The style of the interior (1830-1840) is extremely harmonious. On your way out, stop at the top of the steps for a magnificent view down the Rue Royale toward the Place de la Concorde.

❷ Despalles ★★★
Village Royal, 26, Rue Boissy-d'Anglas, 75008.
☎ 01.49.24.05.65.
Mon. to Sat. 10am-7pm.

On one side, the Village Royal, 100 square feet of plants, garden furniture and outdoor items for terraces and gardens. On the Boissy-d'Anglas side of the street, an interior design shop, with furniture and gifts in the style of the neighbourhood: in other words, chic and pricey.

❸ Hédiard ★★
21, Pl. de la Madeleine, 75008.
☎ 01.43.12.88.88.
Mon. to Sat. 9:30am-9pm.

Step through the door and you'll be transported by the

scents, colours and flavours. Hédiard renovated its shop to offer customers a taste of far-off places. The interior of the tea room upstairs looks something like a transatlantic liner with a 1920s decor.

❹ Hermès ★★★
24, Rue du Faubourg Saint-Honoré, 75008.
☎ **01.40.17.47.17.**
Mon. 10am-1pm, 2:15-6:30pm; Tues. and Sat 10am-6:30pm.

Everything in the Hermès shop is meant to please the eye, starting with the window displays. Take a look around the different departments: saddles, leather goods, jewellery and clothes. You can spend hours looking through the bags, boots and plaids of the Hermès collection that stretch from one floor to another. The traditional Hermès scarf costs a mere 1,390 francs, but you can buy a beautiful deck of cards for only 200 francs.

❺ Crillon Hotel ★★
10, Place de la Concorde, 75008. ☎ **01.44.71.15.00.**
M° Concorde.

Don't be put off by the name or reputation of this luxury hotel: every afternoon, from 3:30 to 7pm, an excellent harpist

HÔTEL DE CRILLON
PARIS

creates a marvellous ambiance in the Winter Garden tea room. Order a 30-franc coffee and enjoy.

❻ Bernardaud Tea Room ★★
Galerie Royale, 9, Rue Royale, 75008.
☎ **01.42.66.22.55.**
Mon. to Sat. 8:30am-7pm.

This is the place to go to escape the noise of the city. The walls are the colour of the green-tea ice cream served in Japan. Lovely alcoves display examples of fine porcelain created by Bernardaud.

And in this supremely elegant tea room, you not only choose your tea; you also select the design of the cup in which your tea is served.

LUXURY WINDOW SHOPPING

A long with the Avenue Montaigne, this neighbourhood is the heart of Paris luxury goods, with Italian (Cerruti, Gucci, Versace), American (Ralph Lauren, among others) and French designers side by side. The arcades, windows and passages, not to mention the Madeleine itself, have been renovated. The Christmas decorations are often splendid.

❼ Territoire ★★★
30, Rue Boissy-d'Anglas, 75008. ☎ **01.42.66.22.13.**
Mon. to Sat. 10:30am-7pm.

This building, the former Hôtel de Lully, has been classified a historical monument. It's a treasure trove where you can find just about anything, including books, clothes, games, stationery and pens, dishes and woven baskets.

The Palais-Royal,
a historical garden

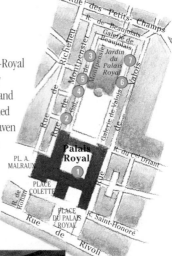

Step through the gates of the Palais-Royal and the noise and bustle of the city disappear as if by magic. The garden and arcades, where the royalty was abolished and the Revolution begun, create a haven of peace. Shops have lined the garden since the 18th century, but the stamp dealers and stores selling miniature lead soldiers have been replaced by clothing and interior design boutiques, which are sheltered discreetly underneath the arches.

❶ Palais-Royal ★★★
Pl. du Palais-Royal, 75001.

Richelieu constructed this architectural complex in 1636, then Louis XIV gave it to his brother, the duc d'Orléans, in 1692. In the 18th century, Philippe Égalité hired the architect Louis to design the pavilions and arcades we see today. He then sold them to shopowners. Gambling halls, restaurants and late-night cafés were haunted by prostitutes and political rabble-rousers who wanted to overturn the monarchy.

❷ À Marie Stuart ★
3, 4, 5, Galerie de Montpensier, 75001.
☎ **01.42.96.28.25.**
Mon. to Fri. 9am-6:30pm, Sat. to 5:45pm.

A wonderful, tiny shop with a 19th-century varnished wood counter, where customers once came for funerary items made from jet and black onyx. It's now a good place to find medals, decorations and badges.

❸ Maison de Vacances ★★
63, 64, Galerie de Montpensier, 75001.
☎ 01.47.03.99.74.
Tues. to Fri. 1-7pm (6pm in winter), Sat. noon-6pm.

Everything is white and lovely in this shop that specialises in table and house linen: embroidered and openwork

linen, lace trompe-l'œil painted on the mirrors; marble powder rubbed over workshop tables. Wool and cashmere cushions for 500 francs.

❹ Didier Ludot ★★
20, 24, Galerie de Montpensier, 75001.
☎ 01.42.96.06.56.
Mon. to Sat. 10:30am-7pm.

A highly recommended shop: Didier Ludot finds haute-couture clothes and accessories, which he then sells for 50 per cent of the original price. The high-class brand names include Chanel, Dior, Balmain, Balenciaga, Hermès (for the Kelly bag and accessories).

❺ L'Escalier d'Argent ★★
42, Galerie de Montpensier, 75001.
☎ 01.40.20.05.33.
Tues. to Sat. 1-7pm.

This antique dealer has a passion for the 18th century, reflected in the hand-cut, handmade vests (starting at 1,400 francs). She uses precious silks, velvets, brocades, and period or re-reprinted fabrics to create these luxury items.

❻ The Salons du Palais-Royal Shiseido ★★★
142, Galerie de Valois, 75001.
☎ 01.49.27.09.09.
Mon. to Sat. 9am-7pm.

Serge Lutens created a setting of purples and violets in which to present the exclusive perfumes produced by Shiseido. Panels painted with 18th-century designs, with a frieze decorated with insects,

suns and moons, surround a spiral staircase with bronze fittings. It's worth stopping by to take a look.

❼ Muriel Grateau ★★
130, 133, Galerie de Valois, 75001.
☎ 01.40.20.90.30.
Mon. 2-7pm, Tues. to Sat. 11am-7pm.

One of the most sophisticated design shops in Paris, where you can find solid colour or damask linens in

a seemingly infinite range of subtle tones, displayed on wrought-iron furniture. Objects for the table, bedroom and bathroom. Tablecloths and mats to go with a selection of delicate glass, flatware, plates and serving dishes.

Around the Place des Victoires
a fashion Mecca

The harmony and the symmetry of the 17th-century architecture creates a perfect showcase for the designer boutiqes that have moved into buildings designed by Hardouin-Mansart, the architect of Versailles. Kenzo, Cacharel, Esprit, Victoire, Mugler and Kelianont found the location that best reflects their styles, making this *Place* and the nearby streets a must-see for shoppers. It's also a favourite hang-out for journalists and designers. At day's end, it is once again a quiet neighbourhood.

❶ The galerie Véro-Dodat ★★★
19, Rue Jean-Jacques-Rousseau, 75001.

The only thing that's disappeared over the years is the original owner; everything else, including the black-and-white tiled floor, the curved windows with copper frames and mirrored pilasters, are still in place. Check out the window displays as you stroll by the

Galerie du Passage, Capia, Il Bisonte, the publishers FMR and Eric Philippe, then take a break at the Époque café.

❷ Anna Joliet, music boxes ★★
9, Rue de Beaujolais, 75001. ☎ 01.42.96.55.13. Tues. to Sat. 10am-7pm, Mon. 2-7pm.

This tiny shop located in Colette's former building is worth seeing even if you aren't a specialist: melodies from hundreds of different music boxes (for children and collectors alike) fill the air. Prices for music boxes start at 200 francs.

❸ Notre-Dame des Victoires

Notre-Dame des Victoires reflected the piety of the common people, as reflected in the moving ex-votoes that cover the walls and pillars. Built to commemorate the conquest of La Rochelle from the Protestants, the church was completed in 1740. During the Revolution, it was used as a commodities exchange.

❹ La galerie Vivienne ★★★

4, Rue des Petits-Champs, 75001.

Some of the boutiques lining the glass-roofed passage have remained unchanged since the 19th-century, when they first opened. The past and present create a lovely blend in the many shops lining the Galerie Vivienne: vases by Emilio Robba, petit-point pillows and rugs at the Casa Lopez, rope furniture by Christian Astuguevieille, sunglasses at Cutler & Gross and designer boutiques.

❺ Peter Hadley ★★

6 bis, Pl. des Petits-Pères, 75001.
☎ 01.42.86.83.73.
Mon. to Sat. 10am-7pm.

Neither the storefront, nor the name, "La Maison Bleue", painted over the door of the shop opposite the Notre-Dame des Victoires Church have changed. But the religious objects have disappeared, replaced by chic sportswear designed for travel and adventure.

❻ Ventilo ★★

27 bis, Rue du Louvre, 75001. ☎ 01.42.33.18.67.
Mon. noon-7pm, Tues. to Sat. 10:30am-7pm.

Three floors for a complete day of shopping: women's clothes designed in a natural, fluid style; a home-design shop for Provençal quilts, pillows, lamps, and perfumes; and finally, a tea room for lunch, where you can collapse into honey- or lavender-coloured rattan chairs.

❼ A Priori Thé ★★

35, Galerie Vivienne, 75001.
☎ 01.42.97.48.75. Mon. to Fri. 9am-6pm, Sat. 9am-6:30pm, Sun. 12:30-6:30pm.

This tea room owes much of its great charm to the light, the location, the summer sun and the glass-roofed terrace. The

staff and clientele are international; the menu, English and American, with brownies and crumbles. It's a favourite with journalists and fashion folk, and a good place for a weekend family outing.

The Louvre and the Tuileries,
a pair of museums

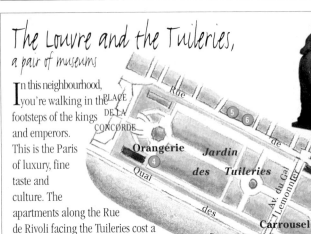

In this neighbourhood, you're walking in the footsteps of the kings and emperors. This is the Paris of luxury, fine taste and culture. The apartments along the Rue de Rivoli facing the Tuileries cost a fortune, the jewellery shops display their treasures against the magnificent backdrop of the Place Vendôme, the Louvre is around the corner, and antique stores and bookshops are everywhere.

❶ Louvre Museum ★★★

Métro: Palais-Royal-Musée du Louvre, enter through the Passage Richelieu.
☎ 01. 40.20.51.51. 9am-6pm; Wed. and Mon. to 9;45pm; closed Tues. Entrance fee.

A full week is barely enough time to see the museum, but if you can only make one trip, don't miss the restored areas of the Grand Louvre: the Cour Marly and 18th-century sculpture, the Cour Khorsabad and Assyria, the Michelangelo Gallery, the former stables of Napoleon III and the medieval Italian sculpture.

For a look at the earliest vestiges of the Louvre, walk around the impressive keep built by Charles V.

❷ Café Marly ★★

93, Rue de Rivoli, Passage Richelieu, 75001.
☎ 01.49.26.06.60.
Daily 8am-2am.

There's no better place to contemplate the illuminated pyramid or enjoy lunch than in the Napoleon III rooms and gallery, renovated by Olivier Gagnère et Yves Taralon into one of the most chic Parisian meeting places. Brunch on Sundays.

❸ Carrousel du Louvre ★★

99, Rue de Rivoli, 75001.
☎ 01.43.16.47.47. Shops open 9am-8pm; closed Tues. Restaurants daily to 11pm.

Forty shops (all open Sunday), restaurants, and fast-food joints: there's something for everyone, from Lalique to the Virgin Megastore and Rooming. A special recommendation for Nature et Découverte (environmentally friendly store) for kids and adults, and for the shop of the Postal Museum, where writing is considered an art.

❹ The Tuileries Gardens ★★★

With 700 newly planted trees and a garden restored to Le Nôtre's 17th-century design, the Tuileries Gardens will soon reflect its original royal lustre. Don't miss the Musée de l'Orangerie facing Concorde ☎ 01. 42.97.48.16. Daily 9:45am-5:15pm.

NOT TO BE MISSED IN THE PAINTING DEPARTMENT OF THE LOUVRE MUSEUM

The intense *Cheater With the Ace of Diamonds* by Georges de La Tour; Vermeer's *Lacemaker*, who seems to be sitting right next to you; *Gilles* by Watteau, filled with a nostalgic ambiance of 18th-century festivities; and the opulent, romantic and exuberant works by Delacroix. These exceptional works are masterpieces of emotion and spirit.

(entrance fee),one of the best places to see works by Soutine and Modigliani. If that's not enough to tempt you, Monet's *Water Lilies* certainly will.

❺ Inter-Continental Hotel ★★
3, Rue de Castiglione, 75001. ☎ 01 44 77 11 11.

After visiting the Louvre and the Tuileries, stop by the terrace of the ultrachic Inter-Continental Hotel (known as the "Interconti" by Parisian snobs). Don't be intimidated by the opulence: you can enjoy a café on the patio for 30 francs.

❻ Galignani ★★
224, Rue de Rivoli, 75001, ☎ 01.42.60.76.07. Mon. to Sat. 10am-7pm.

Founded in 1802, the Galignani publishers became a reading room with foreign newspapers that were unavailable anywhere else. With its 1930 woodwork

and long rows of books in French and English, today's Galignani still retains its unique and charming ambiance. It's one of the best bookshops in Paris for literature, and has a large stock of art, architecture and history books.

❼ Louvre des Antiquaires ★★
2, Pl. du Palais-Royal, 75001. ☎ 01.42.97.27.00. Tues. to Sun. 11am-7pm; closed Sun. (July and Aug.)

You'll probably pay top prices, but if you can't find what you want here, you probably won't find it anywhere. Shops sell furniture, paintings, objets d'art and sculptures from every period. Don't miss the jewellery market in the basement.

Louvre des Antiquaires

Faubourg Saint-Germain,
in Proust's footsteps

This is an old aristocratic neighbourhood in the shadow of the Invalides, where the most beautiful houses are often hidden in courtyards amid unexpected and vast gardens. The streets are quiet, elegant and crowded with the bustle of cars ferrying ministers around Paris. The storefronts are all tastefully harmonised with the 17th- and 18th-century facades. Without the antique dealers, booksellers and decorators, this neighbourhood would lose much of its charm.

❶ The Invalides ★★★

Place des Invalides, 75007.
☎ 01.44.42.37.67.
Daily 10am-6pm.
Entrance fee.

The facade, the main courtyard and the Saint-Louis de Libéral Bruant Church make this one of the architectural masterpieces of the 18th century. If military paraphernalia is your thing, don't miss the museum, which has one of the best collections in the world of weapons and armour, each one of which is a work of art. End your visit with Napoleon's tomb, situated directly under Jules Hardouin-Mansart's dome.

❷ The Orsay Museum ★★★

Parvis, Rue de Bellechasse, 75007.
☎ 01.40.49.48.14.
10am-6pm, Thurs. to 10pm; closed Mon. Entrance fee.

This is the Paris temple of 19th-century art and design.

The collection of Impressionist paintings is exceptional, and several masterpieces recently have been acquired by the museum, including Courbet's *Origin of the World,* until now jealously guarded in private collections; *Starry*

3 THE CARRÉ RIVE GAUCHE

The cream of the Paris antique dealers are located within an area bordered by the Quai Voltaire, the Rue des Saints-Pères, the Rue de l'Université and the Rue du Bac. The furniture, objects and paintings are often of exceptional quality. The Carré exhibits its masterpieces in May, and crowds gather round to window-shop and to enjoy the glitter.

Night by van Gogh; Renoir's *Reclining Nude* and *Portrait of Fernand Halphen*; and a mahogany writing desk by Henry van de Velde. Tea room, restaurant, bookshop, and a museum shop with reproductions of artwork.

4 The Maillol Museum ★★★
61, Rue de Grenelle, 75007.
☎ 01.42.22.59.58.
11am-6pm; closed Tues. and holidays.

The former Bouchardon *hôtel*, where Musset once lived, now houses the collection of Dina Vierny, Maillol's last model. It includes lesser-known aspects of the artist's work, including paintings and tapestries. His pastels and chalk sketches are masterpieces.

5 Siècle ★★
24, Rue du Bac, 75007.
☎ 01.47.03.48.03.
Mon. to Sat. 10:30am-7pm.

Here, each object is treated as if it were one of a kind—and it often is. Ornate designs decorate the silverware, the glasses rest on stems formed of Bacchus figures, and the plates seem to contain the elegance of centuries past.

6 Au Nom de la Rose ★★
46, Rue du Bac, 75007.
☎ 01.42.22.08.09. Mon. to Sat. 9am-9pm, candied petals from 10 to 45 francs.

This sun-filled boutique is overflowing with rose petals: they're on the linen, the pillows, the scarves and the jewellery. You can find rose-scented candles, candied rose petals and, behind a wrought-iron doorway, the garden—filled with old roses.

7 Bonpoint ★★
86, Rue de l'Université, 75007. ☎ 01.45.51.46.28.
Mon. to Sat. 10am-7pm.

The Bonpoint shop was remodelled in keeping with a contemporary image: small educational or poetic gifts, hidden in gauze or

embroidered linen pouches, are slipped in between clothing in the linen-covered baskets. The women's boutique is at 67, Rue de l'Université (☎ 01.45.51.53.18).
Try on the linens, silks and velvets in the lovely fitting rooms decorated with a wrought-iron and crystal chandelier.

8 Les Nuits d'Été ★★
22, Rue de Beaune, 75007.
☎ 01.47.03.92.07.
Daily 11am-7pm, Sun. to 4pm.

A discreet and cosy setting where locals come to meet and editors from the nearby publishing houses get together. Friendly and hospitable. Brunch on Sundays.

Saint-Germain-des-Prés,
the spirit of the Left Bank

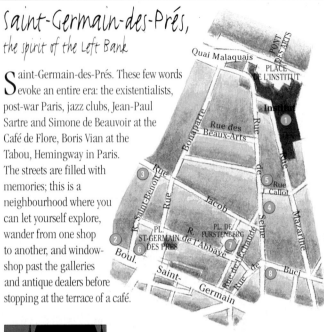

Saint-Germain-des-Prés. These few words evoke an entire era: the existentialists, post-war Paris, jazz clubs, Jean-Paul Sartre and Simone de Beauvoir at the Café de Flore, Boris Vian at the Tabou, Hemingway in Paris. The streets are filled with memories; this is a neighbourhood where you can let yourself explore, wander from one shop to another, and window-shop past the galleries and antique dealers before stopping at the terrace of a café.

❶ The Institut of France ★★★
23, Quai de Conti, 75006.

The illustrious Académie Française meets under the dome built by Le Vau, in the former collège des Quatre Nations founded by Mazarin. Through the cardinal's bequest, the city of Paris acquired a vast library and one of its most beautiful 17th-century buildings. The two curving wings facing the Seine give the building a rather Roman appearance.

❷ Shu Uemura ★★
176, Blvd Saint-Germain, 75006.
☎ 01.45.48.02.55.
Mon. 11am-7pm, Tues. to Sat. 10am-7pm.

With some 100 different shades of make-up, lipstick eyeshadown and blusher, this shop will have what you want; if not, it probably doesn't exist.

Beauticians make up one side of your face, you finish up the other side and carry home a sketch describing how to do it all by yourself. It's practical and useful.

❸ Triff Gallery ★★
35, Rue Jacob, 75006.
☎ 01.42.60.22.60.
Mon. 2:30-7pm, Tues. to Sat. 10:30am-7pm.

A trip to the Middle East that starts in Paris, at the end of a tree-lined avenue. The carpets are strewn around the floor in a lovely and colourful chaos. A fountain in the middle of the gallery makes you feel as if you're in a Syrian palace. The decor itself is worth the trip, not to mention the kilims, and old books and fabrics.

❹ Au Fond de la Cour ★★
49, Rue de Seine, 75006.
☎ 01.43.25.81.89.
Mon. to Sat. 11am-7pm.

The boutique overflows into the courtyard, where the rattan and wrought-iron furniture have taken on a unique sheen. Inside, the shop looks like one of Napoleon III's greenhouses, with curios, sculpted lamps and chandeliers decorated with flowers and foliage reflected in the many mirrors. A lovely place to shop, even if you leave empty-handed.

❺ La Palette ★★
43, Rue de Seine, 75006.
☎ 01.43.26.68.15.
Mon. to Sat. 8am-2am.

This must be one of the most Parisian of all cafés. In rain or shine, summer or winter, the tables are out on the sidewalk. Enjoy a glass of wine in the company of gallery dealers, models and actors. La Palette is a neighbourhood institution; without it, Saint-Germain wouldn't be the same.

❻ The cafés along the Boulevard Saint-Germain ★★★
At 172, LE CAFÉ DE FLORE.
☎ 01.45.48.55.26.
At 170, LES DEUX MAGOTS.
☎ 01.45.48.55.25.
Daily 7:30am-1:30am.

Which one? You don't have to choose, try them both. Early in the morning, a breakfast at the Deux Magots,

❼ THE PLACE FURSTENBERG ★★★

This charming tiny square appears in the middle of the Rue Furstenberg like a stage setting, complete with an iron lamppost and park bench. It's so perfect, it's hard to believe that cameras aren't filming. The Delacroix Museum, where the artist lived and worked, is at 6, Rue Furstenberg (☎ 01.44.41.86.50).

facing the church, is a moment of pure bliss and tranquillity. In the afternoon, the sunlit terraces are equally crowded. And either one displays enough well-known figures to convince you that you're in the right place.

❽ Buci Market ★★
At the intersection of the Rue de Buci and the Rue de Seine. Daily except Mon.

This is *the* Left Bank market, especially on Sundays, when the streets are packed with a particularly Parisian clientele crowding around the heaps of fruits and vegetables. Even if you're not here for your weekly provisions, it's a great place to explore.

The Place Saint-Sulpice and the Carrefour de l'Odéon

The plaster saints have gradually disappeared from the *Place,* along with the religious art shops, but the Visconti Fountain continues to flow undisturbed and the pigeons still land on the towers of the church. Several charming streets (Rue Servandoni and Rue Férou) lead to the Luxembourg Gardens. The Rue Guisarde and the Rue des Canettes, both centuries old, lead past restaurants and shops to the bustle of the Boulevard Saint-Germain.

❶ Saint-Sulpice Church ★★★
Place Saint-Sulpice, 75006.

Walk past the Servandoni facade and go straight to the frescoes painted by Delacroix (1849-1861). To the right of the immense nave, Jacob is still battling the angel, while on the opposite wall, *Heliodorus Expelled from the Temple* depicts the Syrian at the base of a staircase, under a swirl of fabric in the midst of piles of gold and silver.

❷ Avant-Scène ★★
4, Pl. de l'Odéon, 75006.
☎ **01.46.33.12.40.**
Tues. to Sat. 10:30am-1pm, 2-7pm.

"Avant" as in avant-garde, "scène" as in a stage set: for designers who share Élisabeth Delacarte's taste for Baroque and Art Deco, and a determination to abandon the sharp-edged style of the 1980s. Their names: Garouste and Bonetti, Van der Straeten, Dubreuil, Brazier-Jones. Don't hesitate to come in for a look around.

❸ Maison de famille ★★
29, Rue Saint-Sulpice, 75006.
☎ **01.40.46.97.47.**
Mon. to Sat. 10:30am-7pm.

The two floors of this shop make it look like a real home. The gentle and natural colours set the tone. All the furniture has a past and even the smallest object seems somehow familiar. Table linen, dishware,

❹ PLANTS AND FLOWERS

If you follow the Rue Saint-Sulpice to the Carrefour de l'Odéon, you'll walk right in front of the windows of Christian Tortu's shop. And just like everyone else, you'll have to stop and take a look at the incredibly lovely, sophisticated flower and plant arrangements. This is one of the best places for flowers in Paris.

Western House is constantly adding to its vast and exclusive inventory, one worth crossing Paris for.

glasses and clothes all have a certain discreet, bourgeois charm. Plates from 25 francs.

❺ Western House ★
23, Rue des Canettes, 75006.
☎ 01.43.54.71.17.
Mon. 10am-7pm; Tues. to Sat. 10am-7:15pm.

This is where to outfit yourself as a cowboy. You'll find jeans, boots, belts, chequered shirts and cowboy hats— all imported from America over the past 33 years.

❻ Casa Bini ★★
36, Rue Grégoire-de-Tours, 75006.
☎ 01.46.34.05.60.
Mon. to Fri. 12:30-2:30pm, 7:30am-11pm; Sat., Sun. 7:30-11pm. Menu at 250-350 francs.

Anna Bini arrived from Florence with her bags packed with olive oil and delicious products such as poivrades artichokes. Her shop was an immediate success; Parisians love the simplicity of her dishes tinged with the flavours of Tuscany.

❼ Le café de la Mairie ★★
8, Pl. Saint-Sulpice, 75006.
☎ 01.43.26.67.82.
Daily 7am-2am; closed Sun.

It's always hard to find a seat to enjoy a coffee or delicious sandwich on this terrace facing the tower of the church. Inside the neon-lit, beige-coloured room, the habitués—local intellectuals, actors, students—stay late into the night.

❽ Tradition renouée ★★
8, Rue de l'Odéon, 75006.
☎ 01.40.51.08.67.
Mon. to Sat. 11:30am-7pm.

Lamps, chandeliers and pillows (from 600 francs and up). Bags, belts and a hundred small fashion or home decorating accessories, all elegantly trimmed in dozens of colours. Here you'll find a haute-couture spirit without the haute-couture prices.

The Latin Quarter,

medieval Paris and the students

The streets overflow with students when classes end, the cafés stay open until late into the nightn and the university bookshops are abuzz with studious activity. Since the Sorbonne was founded in the 13th century, this part of town has been the centre of learning Paris. Occasionally disrupted by demonstrations, it is trying to remain authentic, despite the fast-food restaurants and clothes shops invading the Blvd Saint-Michel.

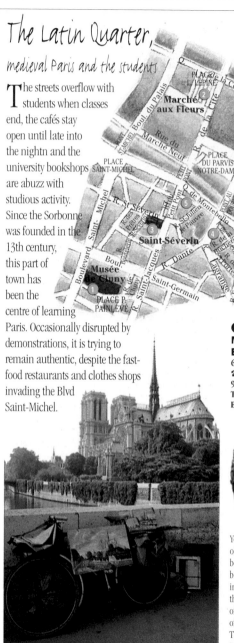

❶ The Cluny Museum and Roman Baths ★★★

6, Pl. Paul-Painlevé, 75005.
☎ 01.53.73.78.00.
9:15am-5:45pm; closed
Tues. and holidays.
Entrance fee.

You'll discover the real history of Paris at the Cluny Museum, beginning with the Roman baths of Lutetia, constructed in the 2nd and 3rd centuries, through the Gothic altar of the Cluny abbeys, a jewel of Flamboyant architecture. The objects come from Parisian monuments of church treasures, and the sculptures evoke the most famous sites in Paris: Saint-Germain, Saint-Denis, the Sainte-Chapelle and Notre-Dame. The museum also houses priceless works from the Middles Ages, including the world-renowned *Unicorn Tapestry,* a reflection of the chivalrous world of courtly love.

❷ THE FLOWER AND BIRD MARKET
Place Louis-Lépine, 75004. Daily 10am-7pm.

This market, a brilliant spot of colour in the heart of the city, is just a few minutes from Notre-Dame Cathedral. On Sundays, the bird market replaces the flowers. You'll feel as if you're in a garden, as you stroll past the different stands, enjoying the scent of a flower of the cry of a mina bird.

❸ Saint-Séverin Church ★★★
Rue des Prêtres-Saint-Séverin, 75005.

This is one of the most beautiful and oldest parish churches in Paris. The development of architectural styles from the 13th century to the 16th century is perfectly

represented, and it is a complete example of the Flamboyant Gothic style. It doesn't take long to visit, but what you see is stunning: the spirals on the central column, the fan vaults and soaring stone.

❹ Shakespeare & Co ★
37, Rue de la Bûcherie, 75005.
☎ 01.43.26.96.50.
Daily noon-midnight.

The bookshelves are overflowing with old and new books, mostly in English; the shop itself is often filled with young Americans abroad. The half-timbered facade just opposite Notre-Dame is one of the oldest in the neighbourhood. There's a tea party every Sunday afternoon on the upper floor in the owner's apartments.

❺ The Tea Caddy ★
14, Rue Saint-Julien-le-Pauvre, 75005.
☎ 01.43.54.15.56.
noon-7pm; closed Wed.

Agatha Christie had already created Hercule Poirot and Miss Marple when this tea room opened in 1928. They would have liked the timeless English decor of the Tea Caddy, complete with dark wood panelling and leaded windows. Conversations are muffled as the clientele tucks into the delicious apple pies, scones and muffins.

❻ Notre-Dame de Paris ★★★
Île de la Cité, 75004.
8:30am-6:45pm; Sat and Sun to 7:45pm.

This cathedral is one of the most beautiful examples of late 12th-century Gothic architecture. The building has, of course, been altered over the years and even abandoned. It was saved from total ruin by Viollet-le-Duc who, under Napoleon III, renovated and restored the monument, always keeping the original Gothic style in mind. Quasimodo had a fabulous view from the towers; be forewarned, you have to climb up nearly 230 feet of steps to reach the top. But it's worth it!

Around the Pantheon,
from Lutetia to Paris

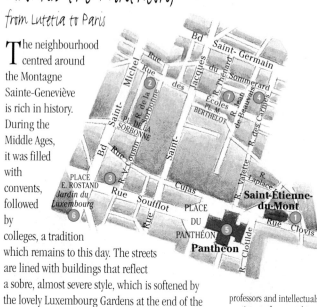

The neighbourhood centred around the Montagne Sainte-Geneviève is rich in history. During the Middle Ages, it was filled with convents, followed by colleges, a tradition which remains to this day. The streets are lined with buildings that reflect a sobre, almost severe style, which is softened by the lovely Luxembourg Gardens at the end of the Rue Soufflot.

❶ The Church of Saint-Étienne-du-Mont ★★★

1, Rue Saint-Étienne-du-Mont, 75005.

This is one of the strangest churches in Paris, completed in the 17th century with an astonishingly asymmetrical Renaissance-style portal. As opposed to most churches, it still has a 16th-century rood. It is an unusually elegant church, with intertwined arches and lacework on the keystones. Pascal and Racine are buried here.

❷ Le Balzar ★★

49, Rue des Écoles, 75005. ☎ 01.43.54.13.67. Daily noon to 1am. Breakfast from 8:30am.

The waiters' outfits haven't changed since 1890: a black vest and white apron. Generations of students, professors and intellectuals continue to frequent this brasserie. Politicos dine side by side with students coming out of the nearby cinemas, with everyone enjoying the traditional French fare.

❸ Dubois ★★

20, 24 Rue Soufflot, 75005. ☎ 01.43.54.43.60. Tues. to Fri. 9:30am-6:30pm; Mon. to Sat. 9:30am-12:30pm, 13:45-6:30.

Colours of all kinds for artists: watercolours, oils and pastels. There's a huge selection, with thousands of different products. Dubois has been doing business in this neighbourhood since 1861.

Consult their phenomenal catalogue for mail orders.

❹ Mayette ★★
8, Rue des Carmes, 75005.
☎ 01.43.54.13.63. Tues. to Sat. 10am-8pm; Sun., Mon. and holidays 2-8pm.

This shop has been in business since 1808 and is the oldest magician's supply store in France. They have every kind of conjurer's trick, from the simplest to the most complex, with demonstrations, cassettes, books, videos and CDROMs, all stashed away in ancient drawers and shelves. It's pure magic.

❺ The Panthéon ★★★
Place du Panthéon, 75005.
☎ 01.44.32.18.00. Daily 10am-6:15pm. Entrance fee.

Louis XV made a vow to construct a church devoted to Saint Geneviève and asked the architect Soufflot to draw up the plans; he then created a church with a Greek cross. A victim of political upheavals and changing governments, the church was transformed into a pantheon, then once again a church until finally, with the death of Victor Hugo, it became the "Resting Place of Great Men". The steps of

visitors echo in the vast nave, decorated with ephemeral frescoes by Puvis de Chavannes.

❻ LUXEMBOURG GARDENS ★★★
An idyllic spot, where Romantic poets and artists often strolled, and a favourite with Parisians. Toy sailing boats still maneuver back and forth on the octagonal pool, the centrepiece of this lovely garden. Take a break from the city: have a seat, read your newspaper and relax.

❼ Au Vieux Campeur ★★
18 shops near 48 Rue des Écoles, 75005.
☎ 01.43.29.12.32. Tues. to Sat. 10:30am-7:30pm; Wed. to 9pm.

If you're looking for any sports equipment, this is the place. The Camper shops can equip you from head to toe for any sport:

hiking, climbing, skiing, swimming, surfing (on water or snow) deep-sea diving and camping. Business has been booming since the shops opened in 1941. Mail-order is available.

Beaubourg,
the world of art and the sideshows

The Place in front of the Centre Georges Pompidou (closed for renovation through the year 2000) is lined with pizza restaurants and take-out joints. Yet the neighbourhood has managed to withstand the crowds of tourists and strollers who have invaded the Place and the nearby streets. The art galleries draw a steady clientele eager to see works by well-known artists. And soon, you'll be able to see the treasures in the collection of the Modern Art Museum, one of the world's best.

❶ Le quartier de l'Horloge

This real-estate development, constructed on the Beaubourg Plateau, has not been a great success, and there's not much to see in the small paved courtyards and passages. But you might want to take a look at "The Defender of Time", a strange automaton which, at a specific time, wages a mechanical battle against his metallic enemies. Nearby, the Perles Box boutique offers an immense selection of beads of all sorts (glass, metal, shell and so on). It's a perfect place to make the bracelets and necklaces you need to re-create a neo-sixties look, or decorate your T-shirts. You can purchase a necklace kit starting at 57 francs.

❷ The Café Beaubourg ★★
100, Rue Saint-Martin, 75004.
☎ 01.48.87.63.96.
Daily 8am-1am; Fri. and Sat. to 2am.

An invisible boundary seems to protect this café from some of the down-and-out people who've taken up residence on the Place. The architecture by Christian de Portzamparc (who designed the Music Museum at La Villette) is ageing well; this post-modernistic temple seems untouched by time.

❸ Dame Tartine ★
2, Rue Brisemiche, 75004.
☎ 01.42.77.32.22.
Daily noon-11pm.

Come here to join up with a trendy, rather artistic and intellectual crowd, which gathers in the afternoons or evenings on the Place facing the fountain where Niki de Saint-Phalle and Jean Tinguely created their serpents and Mae West mouths spewing water to the sky. Paintings decorate the wall, as befits the neighbourhood.

❹ Beaubourg Gallery ★★
23, Rue du Renard, 75004.
☎ 01.42.71.20.50.
Tues. to Sat. 10:30am-1pm, 2-7pm.

This is the world of Marianne and Pierre Nahon: one of the first galleries to have moved to the area around the Centre Pompidou. It is a reference in the contemporary art market. The Beaubourg Gallery exhibits paintings and sculptures by Arman, Ben, César, Klein and Andy Warhol.

❺ Neotu Gallery ★★
25, Rue du Renard, 75004.
☎ 01.42.78.91.83.
Mon. to Sat. 10am-7pm.

This is where to go to see a piece of designer furniture and to get a look at what's in the

forefront of modern design. Pierre Staudenmeye exhibits limited editions by Garouste and Bonetti, Olivier Gagnère, Martin Szekely on the two floors of his gallery. It is definitely worth making a trip to see this gallery.

❻ The Maeght Gallery ★★
12, Rue Saint-Merri, 75004.
☎ 01.42.78.43.44.
Tues. to Sat. 10am-1pm, 2-7pm.

❼ ECLACHE & CIE
10, Rue Saint-Merri, 75004. ☎ 01.42.74.62.62.
Daily noon-1am.

Here's a perfect Parisian restaurant for a pleasant break at lunch or dinner. In the summer, tables are placed outside in the adjacent passage. The clientele includes lots of young, trendy folk. Brunch is served on Saturday and Sunday (8:30am-noon) for 100 francs. A full meal with wine is about 140 francs.

A 17th-century building is the backdrop for this world-famous gallery. Most of the greatest modern artists, from Braque to Calder, Del Rey, Giacometti and Tapiès, have exhibited their works on these walls. Great bookshop too.

Niki de Saint-Phalle fountain on the Place Igor Stravinsky

Saint-Eustache and Les Halles,
the heart of Paris

Saint-Eustache
PLACE
R. CASSIN

The neighbourhood of Les Halles is once again a place with a great street scene. Things may not get started as early as before, but tend to go on later into the night. Many of the old buildings have been saved and restored, and now house trendy clothes shops of all kinds. On Saturday and Sunday mornings, locals get their marketing done, stopping for a drink or café with friends, in an authentic Parisian ambiance.

❶ Saint-Eustache Church ★★★
2,4, Impasse Saint-Eustache, 75001.

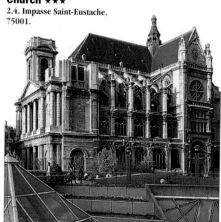

This is a treasure both for its Renaissance architecture and for its history. Richelieu was baptised here, Louis XIV celebrated his first communion, and Colbert and Rameau are buried within its walls. Berlioz first performed his *Te Deum* here; Liszt, his *Messe de Gran*. A concert is played every day, in the late morning or afternoon, on the great organ, one of the largest in Paris. The concert schedule is posted every day on the door of the church.

❷ Dehillerin ★
18, Rue Coquillière, 75001.
☎ 01.42.36.53.13.
Mon. 8am-12:30pm, 2-6pm;
Tues. to Sat. 8am-6pm.

It's best to get up early and set off for Dehillerin before the busloads of Japanese tourists arrive. Somewhere, between the ground floor and the basement, you will find

absolutely every possible kitchen device you need, and probably many that you don't! The shop has a huge selection of copper, cast-iron and aluminium pots and pans.

❸ Le Centre Ville ★★
57, Rue Montorgueil, 75002.
☎ 01.42.33.20.40.
Daily 8am-8pm; Sun. 9am-1pm; closed Mon.

This is one of those Paris bistros featured in the films from the 1950s, with slightly smoked-stained beige walls and a mahogany counter. There are just a few tables, occupied by locals and the usual trendy bunch, where everyone eats elbow to elbow.

❹ Kiliwatch ★
64, Rue Tiquetonne, 75002.
☎ 01.42.21.17.37.
Mon. to Sat. 11am-7pm.

Here's where to find everything that glitters and glows, from princess dresses to dancer's outfits. Fancy lacework, spangles, strass, paillettes,

gilt and kitsch. Not to mention the jeans, striped cottons, plaids and New Age prints.

❺ La Droguerie ★
9, Rue du Jour, 75001.
☎ 01.45.08.93.27.
Mon. 2-6:45pm; Tues. to Sat. 10:30am-6:45pm.

A delicious assortment of colours with skeins of wool, linen, cotton and mohair

covering the walls. Plus ribbons, beads and feathers. And thousands of buttons, including old ones and unusual designs (from 0.50 to 150 francs). Braids, spangles and all kinds of ribbons.

❻ Stohrer ★
51, Rue Montorgueil, 75002.
☎ 01.42.33.38.20.
Daily 7:30am-8:30pm.

❼ AGNÈS B. ★★
2, 3, 6, 10, Rue du Jour, 75001. Children, women's wear (☎ 01.45.08.56.56); men, travel items. Mon. to Sat. 10am-7:30pm.

The Agnès B style is simple, fashionable and contemporary. Her classic clothes, from jeans to shirts, dresses and skirts, are mostly in basic colours: white, black, beige. The art gallery at 8, Rue du Jour (☎ 01.42.33.43.40, Tues to Sat. 10am-7pm)is a place where Agnès B gives young artists a chance to exhibit contemporary painting, sculpture and especially photography.

This shop has been in business since 1730! Stohrer arrived in France with Marie Leczinska, Louis XV's fiancee. After several years, he moved to the Rue Montorgueil, and his pastry shop was soon the place to find the best *puits d'amour* and *Ali-Baba* in all of Paris. The decor by Paul Baudry is worth the trip alone.

Around Saint-Paul,
where time has stopped

The Île Saint-Louis sits like a ship in the middle of the Seine. It forms a village unto itself in the heart of the city. The quiet river banks, classical façades and Seine riverscape make it a timeless, place. And on the right bank, between the quays and the Saint-Paul Church, is one of the most beautiful walks in the capital, where the streets and buildings carry centuries of history.

Hôtel de Beauvais

Hôtel de Sens

Village Saint-Paul

ÎLE St-LOUIS en l'Île

Hôtel de Lauzun

Hôtel Lambert

PONT DE SULLY

❶ Izrael ★★
30, Rue François-Miron, 75004.
☎ **01.42.72.66.23.**
Tues. to Sat. 9:30am-1pm, 2:30-7pm.

A spice and condiments shop straight out of the Middle East. The piled-up sacks, crates and boxes contain scents and colours from far-off places. All the exotic ingredients you need to flavour your recipes fit, miraculously, in the wonderful chaos of this small shop.

❷ Calligrane ★★
4, 6, 6 bis, Rue du Pont-Louis-Philippe, 75004.
☎ **01.40.27.00.74.**
Mon. to Sat. 11am-7pm.
Different kinds of papers from the world over. There's a great selection: paper inlaid with exotic wood, Japanese paper and parchment (lampshades made to order).

❸ Galerie Sâling ★★
14, Rue de Fourcy, 75004.
☎ 01.40.27.95.75. Mon.
to Sat. 10:30am-8pm; Sun.
1-8pm.

This gallery specialises in crafts from Central Asia. Most of the jewellery, clothes and carpets come from Afghanistan.
The silver rings set with semi-precious stones are magnificent, and some of the Pakistani spice boxes are especially beautiful. Jewellery for every budget, from 100 to 10,000 francs.

❹ Papier + ★★
9, Rue du Pont-Louis-Philippe, 75004.
☎ 01.42.77.70.49.
Mon. to Sat. noon-7pm.

This is one of the first shops of its kind, where paper is treated as an art form: pencils that come in some 70 different colours, notebooks in every shade of the rainbow, recycled paper, and paper products sold by the kilo (80 francs).

❺ Private mansions ★★★
An architectural and historical tour of the neighbourhood's mansions. Queen Margot once lived in the medieval Hôtel de Sens on the Rue du Figuier. The Hôtel de Beauvais on the Rue François-Miron was Mozart's home in 1763. Chopin and Delacroix dined at the Hôtel Lambert (Rue Saint-Louis-en-l'Île). As did Baudelaire and Théophile Gautier at the Hôtel de Lauzun, Quai d'Anjou.

❻ The Saint-Paul Village ★★
23, 25, Rue Saint-Paul, 75004.
Thurs. to Mon. 11am-7pm; closed Tues. and Wed.

An antiquites market, with several shops on the street and in the courtyard.

Le Vicomte, ☎ 01.40.27.94.22. 18th-century furniture and barbotine. Le Puceron Chineur, ☎ 01.42.72.88.20. Silver. La Souris Verte, ☎ 01.42.74.79.76. Linen, lace, glass, knick-knacks. Au Débotté, ☎ 01.48.04.85.20. 18th-century furniture and objects, paintings, sculpted woodwork and giltwood.

❼ Île Saint-Louis ★★★
In the 17th century Île Saint-Louis was considered merely the outskirts of the Marais district. The island still has a village-like atmosphere with quiet streets and peaceful river banks.
A stroll around the island on the quays is lovely at any time of day; even in bad weather you'll still see the most beautiful cityscapes in Paris.
At night, the passing bateaux-mouches illuminate the island for brief, magical moments.

Passe-partout, ☎ 01.42.72.94.94.
Locks and keys, corkscrews, nutcrackers, old knives, everything for writers and smokers.

The Marais, an open-air museum

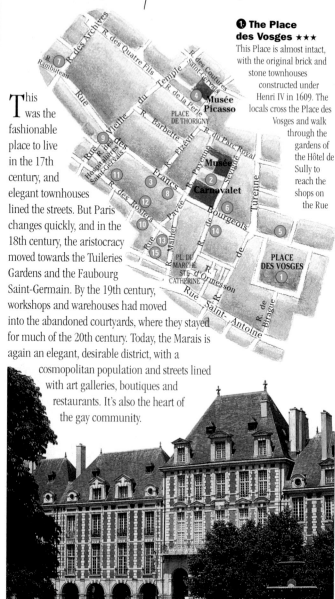

❶ The Place des Vosges ★★★

This Place is almost intact, with the original brick and stone townhouses constructed under Henri IV in 1609. The locals cross the Place des Vosges and walk through the gardens of the Hôtel de Sully to reach the shops on the Rue

This was the fashionable place to live in the 17th century, and elegant townhouses lined the streets. But Paris changes quickly, and in the 18th century, the aristocracy moved towards the Tuileries Gardens and the Faubourg Saint-Germain. By the 19th century, workshops and warehouses had moved into the abandoned courtyards, where they stayed for much of the 20th century. Today, the Marais is again an elegant, desirable district, with a cosmopolitan population and streets lined with art galleries, boutiques and restaurants. It's also the heart of the gay community.

Saint-Antoine. Stroll around the arcade and window-shop in front of the antique stores, bookshops, art galleries and clothing stores. At night, you may feel transported to the time of Victor Hugo, who lived here for many years. This is one of the best walks in Paris.

❷ Carnavalet Museum ★★★

23, Rue de Sévigné, 75003.
☎ 01.42.72.21.13.
10h-17h40, closed Mon.
Entrance fee.

You can go into the courtyard and admire one of the few Renaissance mansions in Paris. The rooms are decorated in 17th- and 18th-

century styles. Explore through the rooms devoted to the history of Paris:

a collection concerning the Revolution, paintings by Hubert Robert and memorabilia of the royal family. End your tour with the 1900 decor designed by Mucha for the jeweller Fouquet. There's also a great book-store and museum shop.

❸ Paris-Musées ★

29 bis, Rue des Francs-Bourgeois, 75004.
☎ 01.42.74.13.02.
Tues. to Sat. 11am-7pm;
Mon. 2-7pm; Sun. 2-6:30pm.

With simple materials—cardboard, grating and painted wood—and great talent, Jean Oddes decorated this shop in a 17th-century style. This is where to find tableware and household objects copied from works in the collections of the City of Paris museum.

❹ Picasso Museum ★★★

Hôtel Salé, 5, Rue de Thorigny, 75004.
☎ 01.42.71.25.21.
9:30am-6pm (April to Sept.), to 5:30pm (Oct. to March); closed Tues.
Entrance fee.

This museum has a large collection representing all of Picasso's work, housed in one of the most beautiful *hôtels* in the Marais. It's a must, if only to see the *Self-Portrait* from his blue period; the *Still Life with Cane Chair* from his Cubist years, and *Pan's Flute*, from his classical period. Picasso's sculptures are represented by the

amazing *Guenon and Child*, as well as the *Young Girl Skipping Rope*. Don't miss the most beautiful Matisse on Paris: *Still Life with Oranges*. The bookshop has a large selection of art books.

❺ Les Deux Orphelines ★★

21, Pl. des Vosges, 75003.
☎ 01.42.72.63.97.
Mon. to Fri. 11am-7pm.

Walk through the door and enter into a world of charming antiques: a turn-of-the-century straw armchair, a light-coloured wood pedestal table, a watercolour of a landscape or a framed bouquet of flowers.

❻ Autour du Monde Home ★
8, Rue des Francs-Bourgeois, 75003.
☎ 01.42.77.06.08.
Mon.-Sat. 11am-7:30pm.

A home store for the natural look, with lots of recycled furniture (American barnwood), antique objects from the United States and Portugal. Classic taste and traditional styles. There are clothes as well: the "basics" collections by Bensimon, in linen and cotton, of course.

❼ Les Mille Feuilles ★★
2, Rue Rambuteau, 75003.
☎ 01.42.78.32.93.
Mon. to Fri. 10am-12:30pm, 1:30-8pm; Sat. to 7pm.

Located on the corner of the Rue des Archives, this enchanting shop draws people from every corner of Paris. Vases and baskets of flowers are scattered on pedestal

tables, garden tables and secondhand chairs. Everything in this lovely disorder is for sale.

❽ Jean-Pierre de Castro ★★
17, Rue des Francs-Bourgeois, 75004.
☎ 01.42.72.04.00.
Tues. to Sat. 10:30am-7pm; Sun. 11am-1pm, 2-7pm; Mon. 2-7pm.

All kinds of silver objects, stacked floor to ceiling. Items from the 17th century through to the 1950s and almost all (90 per cent) secondhand. Flatware, tea and coffee services, and serving dishes as far as the eye can see. Silver-plated forks and spoons are sold by weight. Now's the time to refurbish your table settings!

SUNDAY SHOPPING

The Marais is one of the few neighbourhoods in Paris where most of the shops stay open on Sunday. It's good to know if you still have errands to do before returning home. It's a good idea to check the opening times, because the hours often differ from weekdays. But be forewarned: you won't be alone!

❾ L'Art du Bureau ★
47, Rue des Francs-Bourgeois, 75004.
☎ 01.48 87 57 97.
Mon. to Sat. 10:30am-7pm; Sun. 2-7pm.

The window display stands out on this street mostly given over to clothes shops. Lots of office supplies made of wood, polished pewter and other metals. Files, datebooks, paper cutters, vases and pens, including Mont Blancs, Omas, Recife, Lamy and more.

⑩ L'Éclaireur ★★
3 ter, Rue des Rosiers,
75004.
☎ 01.48.87.10.22.
Tues. to Sat. 11:30am-19h;
Mon. 2-7pm.

L'Éclaireur has managed to
make do quite well with
this former printing shop.
Spread out over two floors are
pieces of designer furniture
covered with items of
clothing for sale. The
styles tend towards the
avant-garde look, and
most of the jewellery,
glass and objects are
signed. This is the
exclusive outlet for
the Italian designer
Fornasetti.

⑪ Chez Marianne ★
2, Rue des Hospitaliers-
Saint-Gervais, 75004.
☎ 01.42.72.18.86.
Daily noon-midnight.

Marianne is on the corner of
the Rue des Rosiers, in the
midst of ready-to-wear clothes
shops and Jewish boutiques.
The walls are lined with
bottles, and near the door is a
delicatessen counter with
boxes of dried fruits and spices.
Paintings over the bar and
Eastern European specialities.

⑫ Hariet
de Prague ★★
6, Rue des Rosiers, 75004.
☎ 01.42.77.15.87.
Tues. to Sat. 11am-6pm.

This is just like a milliner's
shop, where you can find the
perfect little straw hat or
hooded cape covered
with flowers or
feathers, and a
selection of styles
that range from
extravagant to
classical. There
are lovely
wedding dresses,
plus evening
and cocktail
outfits.

⑬ Le Loir
dans la Théière ★★
3, Rue des Rosiers, 75004.
☎ 01.42.72.90.61.
Mon. to Fri. 11:30am-7pm;
Sat., Sun. 9:30am-7pm.

Lewis Carroll would have loved
the English ambiance of this
tea room, where you can spend
hours reading magazines and
newspapers in comfortable old
armchairs set around 1930s or
Henri II tables. Art shows and
delicious pastries.

⑭ Losco ★
20, Rue de Sévigné, 75004.
☎ 01.48.04.39.93.
Tues. to Fri. 11am-1:45pm,
2:30-7pm; Mon. 2-7pm; Sat.
11am-7:30pm.

This the belt shop par excellence.
The decor is all in wood and
lovely tiles and a leather scent
pervades. Losco is a craftsman
who will custom-make a belt
for you as you watch, in the
colour you want and with any
kinds of buckles you choose.

⑮ Caravane ★★★
6, Rue Pavée, 75004.
☎ 01.44.61.04.20.
Thurs., Fri., Sat. 11am-7pm.

The caravan is, quite simply,
a treasure trove: embroidered
wall hangings from Central
Asia; cotton and appliquéd
fabrics from India; carpets
from Morocco starting at 130
francs; Ashanti and Lunda
weavings from Africa; Foutas
from Tunisia for after the bath.

Bastille and the Faubourg Saint-Antoine,
trendy and traditional Paris

A few remaining workshops and craftsmen hidden in the back courtyards still carry on the furniture-building tradition of the *quartier*.

At night, a multitude of bars and restaurants attract a mixed clientele of city- and suburb-dwellers. And each Friday night, hordes of motorcycles converge in front of the Opera on the Place de la Bastille, where they perform their own unique choreography.

Bd Beaumarchais
Boulevard Richard Lenoir
R. Daval
R. de la Bastille
R. St-Antoine
PLACE DE LA BASTILLE
Opéra Bastille
R. du Faubourg Saint-Antoine
Rue de la Roquette
Rue Keller
Rue des Taillandiers
Rue de Lappe
Rue de Charonne
Rue Thiéré
Cour du Bel-Air
Rue de Charenton
Rue de Lyon

❶ Café des Phares ★★
7, Pl. de la Bastille, 75004.
☎ 01.42.72.04.70.
Daily 6:30am-4am.

Italian-style sandwiches and great coffee. Every Sunday morning at 11am the philosopher Marc Marsautet leads an open discussion and debate among a diverse, lively group. It's a popular get-together, so it's best to arrive early, around 10am. Chess, backgammon and jazz on Friday nights. Paintings and photographs on the walls.

❷ Bofinger ★★
3,7 Rue de la Bastille, 75004.
☎ 01.42.72.87.82.
Daily noon-1am.
Lunch menu for 169 and 119 francs.

It used to be open 24 hours a day, when the restaurant first started in 1864. No longer, but this brasserie still maintains the traditions of Bofinger, the original owner. Just about

everyone has eaten here. The interior has been classified a historical site. This is the first place where beer on tap was served. The brasserie food is excellent. It's a bit calmer on the first floor, where you can also admire the frescoes by Hansi.

❸ Jean-Paul Gaultier Gallery ★★

30, Fg Saint-Antoine, 75012.
☎ 01.44.68.84.84.
Mon. 11am-7pm; Tues. to Sat. 10am-7pm.

Pure Gaultier at the Bastille, with three lines of clothings furniture, perfume and a host of odd objects. Televisions and mosaics of the zodiac decorate the floor, while stars of different colours shine from the ceiling. The walls are decorated with métro tiles and trick mirrors. The interior, created by Gaultier himself, is worth the trip alone.

❹ Bastille Opera ★★

Place de la Bastille, 75011.
☎ 01.43.43.96.96.
Reservations
Daily, except Sun. 11am-6pm at ☎ 01.44.73.13.00;
minitel 3615 THEA.

This legacy from the Mitterrand years was controversial from the very start: it was considered too far from the city centre; the architecture by Carlos Ott shocked many; and the acoustic quality of the immense 2,700-seat theatre was questioned. And the early years were difficult, with a series of power struggles, multiple rivalries, differences of opinions, and financial problems. The controversy has died down, and the public is now more interested in the performers, the sets and the quality of the orchestra.

❺ Café du Passage ★★

12, Rue de Charonne, 75012.
☎ 01.49.29.97.64.
Daily 10am-2am;
Sat. noon- 2am.

This is where to find a very late-night snack in a very British bar. Local craftsmen mingle with film-makers and architects at the bar and in the comfortable lounge, furnished with blood-red and saffron-coloured armchairs.

❻ L'arbre à Lettres ★★

62, Fg Saint-Antoine, 75012.
☎ 01.53.33.83.23.
Mon. 1-8pm; Tues. to Sat. 10am-8pm; Sun. 3-7:30pm.

❼ RUE DE LAPPE

The reputation of this street is legendary; it was once a tougher place where Parisian couples spent the night dancing in any one of the many clubs lining the street. The Balajo still has a hint of the old flavour, but what can we say about the Japanese restaurants or Tex-Mex joints?

Somehow, this bookshop managed to slip, surreptitiously, in between two furniture stores. The interior is sobre and discreet, with the exception of the room devoted to art books. It faces the Bel-Air courtyard, one of the most beautiful in the area. The shop hasn't changed since the 19th century.

Rooms and restaurants

There are more than a thousand places to stay in Paris; most are two- and three-star hotels. Choose one in your price range, of course (keeping in mind that Paris is an expensive city, hotels included). And opt for a neighbourhood which best corresponds to what you're looking for in a visit to Paris.

HOTELS

You'll find the international crowd at easy-to-reach places like the Opéra, the Madeleine or the grand boulevards. The Champs-Elysées area is chic and expensive; the 7th, 9th and 16th *arrondissements* are calm and residential; and the Left Bank is younger, livelier and you can find less expensive rooms there.

A double room costs from about 180 to 350 francs in a one-star, 350 to 500 francs in a two-star, and 500 to 800 francs in a three-star hotel. Anything above that can easily cost you more than 800 francs a night. The star ratings are established by the Ministry of Tourism and the Paris Prefecture according to various criteria such as the size of the rooms (12 m2 minimum in a three-star hotel), the comfort, and whether or not there are night porters and bilingual or trilingual staff. Be aware that there is not a single standard which holds from one district to another, or from one hotel to the next.

BOOKING A ROOM

From April through November, you should book your room by phone and confirm by fax or mail, then send a check for the deposit (10 to 15 percent of the price) or give your credit card number: the room will be held for you till 6pm on the day you are due to arrive, or later if you give advance warning. Otherwise the hotel can keep your deposit as compensation for your non-arrival. Except in May, June, September and October, you can try to negotiate the price of a luxury room or get a reduction of 30 to 40 per cent, but you are not sure to succeed. If you visit Paris out of season, but during a major event like the Motor Show or the Agricultural Show, you should also book in advance. The Paris Tourist Office can help you find and book accommodation (see 'Useful numbers' inside the back cover). There is also a centralised hotel reservation service:

☎ 01.43.59.12.12, or Minitel 3616, ELY 1212.

EXTRAS

If you have children, you can ask for an extra bed in a double room or negotiate a suite, but your hotelier will not necessarily allow you to share a room with your poodle. The price of a room does not always include breakfast: expect to pay from 30 to 80 francs depending on the hotel. A TV in your room is a plus, but watch out for those minibars, if you have one: the price of these small bottles adds up quickly and your bill may come as a big surprise.

TOURIST ACCOMMODATION, BED AND BREAKFAST

You can also find tour residences or rooms in private houses (see Tourist Office, 'Useful number', on the inside back cover). *Tourisme chez l'habitant*, 27, Rue Rambuteau, 75004, ☎ 01.34.25.44.44 (a double room with private bathroom for 320-400 francs, breakfast included; you will also have to pay a 50-franc registration fee). Inexpensive accommodation for students and anyone

LATE-NIGHT DINING

Most places stop serving sometime around 10 or 11pm. If you want something to eat later than that, you can try one of the following restaurants, which stay open all night: *La maison d'Alsace*, 39, Champs-Élysées, 75008, ☎ 01.53.93.97.00; *Pied de Cochon*, 6, Rue Coquillière, 75001, ☎ 01.42.36.11.75; *Grand Café*, 4, Blvd des Capucines, 75009, ☎ 01.43.12.19.00. You can also choose from one of the following chains: the *Hippopotamus*, *Le Bistro Romain* and *Léon*, for example, as do many fast-food restaurants. Just don't expect a gourmet's paradise.

else on a tight budget: Résidence Bastille, 151, Ave Ledru-Rollin, 75004, ☎ 01.42.72.72.09; or UCRIF, 27, Rue de Turbigo, 75002, ☎ 01.40.26.57.64. The Centre International de Séjour de Paris, 17, Blvd Kellermann, 75013, ☎ 01.44.16.37.38, is something like a two-star youth hostel, where a double room with breakfast costs 151 francs per person, and a dormitory room for eight, 109 francs per person, breakfast included.

You can also sleep in a tent or park a mobile home in the Bois de Boulogne, at the Allée du bord de l'eau (quite an experience), ☎ 01.45.24.30.00, open all year round.

RESTAURANTS

Paris caters to every price range and all kinds of tastes, including typically French or exotic cuisine, gourmet dishes and hearty regional specialities. You'll find small bistros, lively brasseries and gastronomic restaurants. If the place is well-known, it's wise to call ahead to book your table.

Unfortunately, tourist areas are not always the best places to eat, and you may pay more than the meal is actually worth. Beware, especially in Montmartre, Montparnasse and Les Halles (with a few notable exceptions, of course).

THE BILL, PLEASE

Menu prices always indicate the price per person. Some restaurants have fixed-price menus, which may or may not include drinks (certain menus propose main course plus a glass of wine). The average price of a good meal in Paris is higher than elsewhere in France. It's possible to dine for 70 francs in a simple restaurant, but the price for dinner generally starts from 100 to 120 francs per person.

A 15 per cent service charge is already included in the price, but it is customary to tip the waiter or waitress, especially if the food or service was exceptional. Most restaurants sell cigarettes if you're desperate for a smoke. In top-notch establishments, you can even order your favourite Havana cigar, provided, of course, that your table is in the area reserved for smokers.

Cafés, Bars and Ice-cream

Taverne Henri-IV

13, Pl. du Pont-Neuf, 75001,
☎ 01.43.54.27.90. M° Pont-
Neuf. Noon-9pm, Sat. noon-
4pm; closed Sun. About 80 FF.

Between La Samaritaine and the
Latin Quarter, an excellent place
to stop for a glass of fine wine—
a Beaujolais, Chinon or Morgon
(the proprietor is a connoisseur,
who also bottles some wine himself)—with toast and charcuterie from the Aveyron, or typical
French cheeses.

Berthillon

31, Rue Saint-Louis-en-l'Île,
75004, ☎ 01.43.54.31.61.
M° Pont Marie. 10am-8pm;
closed Mon. and Tues. off
season.

In summertime, you'll have
to queue (especially Sundays),
but it's worth it for the melt-
in-the-mouth ices and sorbets:
try melon, mandarin, raspberry
or pear.

Le Flore en l'Île

42, Quai d'Orléans, 75004,
☎ 01.43.29.88.27.
M° Pont Marie. 9am-2am.

This is the best place to go
if you get a sudden midnight
craving for a cup of tea with
chocolate cake or crème brûlée,
preferably on the Île Saint-
Louis.

Café maure de la Mosquée

38, Rue Geoffroy-Saint-
Hilaire, 75005,
☎ 01.43.31.18.14.
M° Jussieu. Daily 9am-11pm.

It's crowded at weekends, but
you're guaranteed an exotic
change of scene. Sip a glass of
mint tea and soak up the atmosphere: the place is decorated with Moroccan mosaics and
gazelle horns. It costs next to

nothing, and you can relax in
the hammam afterwards.

Harry's Bar

5, Rue Daunou, 75002,
☎ 01.42.61.71.14.
M° Opéra. 10:30am-4am.

An institution dating from 1911,
once frequented by Hemingway
and Fitzgerald. For lovers of pure
malt whisky or fancy cocktails.
You'll almost always find a
lively crowd.

Damman's

20, Rue du Cardinal-
Lemoine, 75005,
☎ 01.46.33.61.30.
M° Cardinal-Lemoine.
To 8pm (midnight in
summer); closed Sun.

According to your mood and
your appetite, you can snack
on a tasty little salad or gorge
on a whole variety of ices.

La Pagode

57 bis, Rue de Babylone,
75007, ☎ 01.45.56.10.67.
M° St-François-Xavier.
4-10pm, Sun. 2-8pm.

An avant-garde movie theatre
with a rich red Chinese decor
where you can also stop for
a slice of apple tart and a cup
of tea in the garden (about
40 francs), especially pleasant
when the weather is fine.

Café Blanc

40, Rue François-1er, 75008,
☎ 01.53.67.30.13. M°
George-V. Sat. 8am-6pm;
closed Sun. and Sat.
Menu 50 FF.

You can't afford a cute little
designer dress? Console yourself with a savoury tart or the
reasonably-priced "dish of the
day".

La Coupole

102, Blvd. Montparnasse,
75006, ☎ 01.43.20.14.20.
M° Vavin. Daily 7:30am-2am.

You can have a drink on the terrace, eat seafood or steak tartare,
take part in an afternoon dance
or pick up a gigolo (if you're
lucky): This famous 1930s brasserie with its painted pillars and
ceiling is still worth a visit, even
if it has lost something of its original charm.

L'Écluse

12-20, Rue François-Ier,
75008, ☎ 01.47.20.77.09.
M° George-V.
Daily 11:30am-1am.

This wine bar is an institution,
though it's a bit pricey. Stop
by for a glass (or bottle) of
Bordeaux, Chateau La Lagune,
Saint-Estèphe, Pauillac or
Saint-Émilion. Have a carpac-
cio or cheese platter with
your drink (58 francs).

HOTELS

Prices are given for double rooms, with or without breakfast. Most have cable television, a minibar and a safe.

Tuileries ★★★
10, Rue Hyacinthe, 75001,
☎ 01.42.61.04.17,
fax 01.49.27.91.56.
M° Tuileries. 690-1,200 FF.

A rarity: a haven of peace behind the Place Vendôme. This restored 18th-century listed building was once the home of Marie-Antoinette's first lady. It has 26 air-conditioned rooms, each with a bathroom, TV, safe, antique furniture and paintings. The service is exceptional, and the guests are likely to be regulars.

Britannique ★★★
20, Ave. Victoria, 75001,
☎ 01.42.33.74.59,
fax 01.42.33.82.65.
M° Chatelet.
762 FF, breakfast: 52 FF.

Forty very comfortable rooms await you here, in a quiet avenue just a stone's throw from the bookstalls along the Seine. This hotel, started in 1840 by the English, still has a British atmosphere with its leather armchairs and Turner reproductions (60 per cent of the guests are American or British). Internet is soon to add a modern touch.

Saintonge ★★★
16, Rue de Saintonge,
75003, ☎ 01.42.77.91.13,
fax 01.48.87.76.41.
M° Rambuteau
or Filles-du-Calvaire.
420-490 FF, breakfast 45 FF.

This hotel, behind the national Archives in the heart of the Marais, has picturesque stone walls, beams and a vaulted breakfast cellar-room, but the comfort is up-to-date and the atmosphere friendly and pleasant.

Pavillon de la Reine ★★★★
28, Pl. des Vosges, 75003,
☎ 01.40.29.19.19,
fax 01.40.29.19.20.
M° Saint-Paul or Bastille.
1,600-2,800 FF.

Step back in time in this idyllic, peaceful hotel, situated in one of the most delightful of Parisian squares, with 55 rooms all overlooking a courtyard or small garden. The atmosphere is one of absolute comfort and *Grand siècle* refinement and sophistication, with wood trim, baldaquins and Louis XIII furniture.

Caron de Beaumarchais ★★★
12, rue Vieille-du-Temple,
75003, ☎ 01.42.72.34.12,
fax 01.42.72.34.63.
M° Hôtel de Ville or St-Paul.
690-770 FF, breakfast 54 FF.

The playwright Beaumarchais used to live near here, and his *Mariage de Figaro* inspired the decoration of the 19 charming air-conditioned rooms: period fabric designs, antique furniture, hand-crafted and painted bathroom tiles. There is also a Louis XVI fireplace in the lounge, and a stone-and-cabochon floor.

Les Deux Îles ★★★
59, Rue Saint-Louis-en-l'Île,
75004, ☎ 01.43.26.13.35.
M° Pont-Marie.
840 FF, breakfast. 47 FF.

This hotel on the Île Saint-Louis has a charm all of its own: 17 small rooms, all soundproofed, with blue-and-white Portuguese-style tiled bathrooms, and Provençal fabrics. There are three basement rooms where breakfast is served.

Notre-Dame ★★★

19, Rue Maître-Albert,
75005, ☎ 01.43.26.79.00,
fax 01.46.33.50.11. M° St-
Michel or Maubert-Mutualité
690-750 FF, breakfast 40 FF.

Thirty-four rooms with antique
furniture (some with exposed
beams and stonework), full bathroom, safe and TV, in a quiet spot
just opposite the cathedral.
There is also a magnificent Aubusson tapestry in the lounge.
And to top it all, the service is ir-
reproachable.

Select ★★★

1, Pl. de la Sorbonne,
75005, ☎ 01.46.34.14.80,
fax 01.45.48.07.86.
M° Luxembourg. 650-890 FF,
buffet breakfast 30 FF.

An original, contemporary decor
in a house with exposed beams
and a central indoor patio with

a glass dome covered in greenery.
There are 67 spacious, air-conditioned rooms, a basement bar
and a waterfall. The hotel is near
the Luxembourg Gardens, perfect for a Sunday morning jog.

Le Clos Médicis ★★★

56, Rue Monsieur-le-Prince,
75006, ☎ 01.43.29.10.80,
fax 01.43.54.26.90.
M° Luxembourg.
790-990 FF, breakfast 60 FF.

This was a private residence in
the late 19th century; today it
is a hotel with 37 air-conditioned
and soundproofed rooms and
duplex suites. There is a hint
of Provence in the stone, wood
and wrought-iron touches,
yellow-ochre tones, bright
fabrics, antique furniture and
tiled bathroom floors. There is
a small garden too: all in all, a

delightful place to stay in the
Latin Quarter.

L'Abbaye ★★★

10, Rue Cassette, 75006,
☎ 01.45.44.38.11,
fax 01.45.48.07.86.
M° Saint-Sulpice. 930-
1,550 FF breakfast included.

Guests are warmly welcomed
in this former convent, now
a charming and quiet hotel.
It has 42 rooms (not very large
but all different and comfortable), a courtyard and garden (pleasant for breakfast
in the summer). An attractive
combination of tradition and
modernity.

Saint-Dominique ★★

62, Rue Saint-Dominique,
75007, ☎ 01.47.05.51.44,
fax 01.47.05.81.28.
M° Invalides. 480-520 FF,
breakfast 40 FF.

A restored 18th-century building (original beams in the reception area) with a summer patio. The 34 rooms have English-style pine furniture. There's a village atmosphere in this neighbourhood; you can spend the morning at the Orsay museum then go shopping in the Opera district or walk over one of the bridges to the Champs-Élysées.

Bersoly's

28, Rue de Lille, 75007, ☎ 01.42.60.73.79, fax 01.49.27.05.55. M° Rue du Bac. 600-750 FF, breakfast 50 FF.

This hotel, in the antique-dealers' area near the Orsay museum, was a convent in the 17th century. The 16 air-conditioned rooms are named after painters (Picasso, Renoir, Lautrec, Gauguin) and are decorated with reproductions of their works. A stone staircase leads down to the vaulted breakfast rooms.

Franklin Roosevelt ★★★

18, Rue Clément-Marot, 75008, ☎ 01.47.23.61.66, fax 01.47.20.44.30. M° Franklin Roosevelt. 795-945 FF, breakfast 65 FF.

In one of the most luxurious areas of the capital, the Franklin Roosevelt is like a private mansion with comfortable lounges and wood trim. The 45 rooms (with bathroom) are decorated in trompe-l'oeil decor, or Japanese-style with cool, springtime tones. Calm and chic.

Hôtel Beau Manoir

6, rue de l'Arcade 75008 Paris - Tél : (1) 42 66 03 07

Beau Manoir ★★★★

6, Rue de l'Arcade, 75008, ☎ 01.42.66.03.07, fax 01.42.68.03.00. M° Madeleine. 1,150 FF with buffet breakfast.

This charming hotel near the Faubourg Saint-Honoré and the department stores has 29 spacious rooms and three suites, with furniture from the Drouot auction rooms. There is a magnificent Aubusson tapestry in the lounge, and an atmosphere of calm and comfort. The buffet-breakfast is served in the vaulted cellars. For about 150 francs, you can enjoy a meal in your room, prepared by student chefs from the Troisgros restaurant.

Lido ★★★

4, Passage de la Madeleine, 75008, ☎ 01.42.66.27.37, fax 01.42.66.61.23. M° Madeleine or Auber. 980 FF with breakfast.

This calm, friendly hotel is quite a find, located so near the noisy streets around the department store area. It has 32 air-conditioned rooms (all with bathrooms), decorated in light-coloured fabrics. You can eat in your room if you wish, and there is a vaulted cellar-room for the buffet-breakfast.

Galileo ★★★

54, Rue Galilée, 75008,
☎ 01.47.20.67.17, fax
01.47.20.66.06. M° George-V.
950 FF, breakfast 50 FF.

An exclusive hotel in an exclusive area. Twenty-seven air-conditioned rooms, decorated in contemporary style, with designer furniture and bathrooms in light-grey marble. For extra comfort, there is a fireplace and a winter garden, with a real garden beyond it.

Tronchet ★★★

22, rue Tronchet, 75008,
☎ 01.47.42.26.14,
fax 01.49.24.03.82.
M° Madeleine.
570-670 FF, breakfast 50 FF.

Right in the heart of Paris, just a stone's throw from the department stores, the Opera district, the theatres, and the bistros in the Rue Daunou. What's more, this hotel has a public car park, a rarity in Paris. The 34 renovated rooms are all tastefully decorated; some even have

exposed beams, and most are air-conditioned. Breakfast is served in the vaulted dining-room, unless, of course, you prefer to have breakfast in bed.

Union Hôtel ★★★

44, Rue Hamelin, 75016,
☎ 01.45.53.14.95,
fax 01.47.55.94.79.
M° Iéna. 715-830 F.
Continental breakfast 45 FF.

Near the Guimet museum and Étoile, this charming, quiet hotel with its 41 rooms has recently been renovated, contemporary-style; all the rooms have a television, minibar and marble bathroom. There is a small indoor garden where you can breakfast in fine weather. The service is always fast.

Pergolèse ★★★★

3, Rue Pergolèse, 75116,
☎ 01.40.67.96.77,
fax 01.45.00.12.11.
M° Argentine. 1,250-1,700 FF,
breakfast 70 and 95 FF.

The interior designer and architect Rena Dumas has left his mark here: the decor is sober and refined, but daring, with a curved glass wall, bright-blue

pillars on sienna walls, light-coloured ash furniture.
Dumas paid careful attention to details in each of the 40 air-conditioned rooms, which all have a lamp, writing desk, mini-bar and television. Beautifully simple and elegant.

RESTAURANTS

Muscade

66, Galerie Montpensier, 75001. ☎ 01.42.97.51.36. M° Palais-Royal. 12:15–21:30pm; closed Sun and Mon. evening. A la carte: 250 FF, Scandinavian menu 198 FF (summer).

Cocteau's apartment, just above this restaurant, inspired the black-and-white marble decor. Gambas, squid, salmon and the "idea or soup of the day". Tea room in the afternoon (delicious chocolate and orange tarts), plus a terrace.

Le Grand Colbert

2-4, Rue Vivienne, 75002. ☎ 01.42.86.87.88. M° Richelieu-Drouot. Daily to noon, valet parking in the evening. Menu 155 FF.

There is a fixed-price menu with a choise three starters, three main courses, three desserts (including the traditional baba) and coffee. The decor hasn't changed since 1830 (note the superb mosaic floor). Expect to pay 200 francs if you order à la carte. Recommended: grilled cod with truffle purée, salmon and salted beef. And for a special night, order a half-litre carafe of champagne!

Aux Pains Perdus

9, Rue du 29-Juillet, 75001, ☎ 01.42.61.17.07. M° Tuileries. 9am-5pm; Sun. and Sat. 11am-5pm. 40-70 FF.

After spending all your money buying jewellery at the nearby Place Vendôme, a light lunch is just what you need! Try a delicious fresh sandwich made with a baguette or speciality breads. The French toasts that give the place its name are not, however, particularly tasty.

Ambassade d'Auvergne

22, Rue du Grenier-Saint-Lazare, 75003. ☎ 01.42.72.31.22. M° Étienne Marcel. noon-2pm, 7:30-10pm. Gourmet menu 170 FF, à la carte 230 FF.

It's unusual to find traditional specialities from the Auvergne in a Parisian restaurant. Try this noisy, friendly place after visit-

ing the neigbourhood around Beaubourg. They serve good, filling dishes like cassoulet with lentils, blood sausage with chestnuts, tripe and so on.

Brin de Zinc...

50, Rue Montorgueil, 75002, ☎ 01.40.21.10.80. M° Les Halles. To midnight, closed Sun. Menu: 180-250 FF.

An atmospheric place full of bric-a-brac, with a great bar. The streetwalkers in the Rue Montorgueil won't distract you from the homemade dishes: calf's head or zucchini gratin.

La Mule du Pape

8, Rue du Pas-de-la-Mule, 75003, ☎ 01.42.74.55.80. M° Chemin Vert. Daily 11am-11pm, closed Sun. night.

For brunch, lunch or dinner near the Place des Vosges in a beige-and-red decor. Large, tasty salads (55-60 francs), eggs Florentine or scrambled, curried casserole, lemon chicken, veal with herbs. Everything is home-made and tastes of the south of France.

Jo Goldenberg

7, Rue des Rosiers, 75004,
☎ 01.48.87.20.16.
M° St-Paul. Daily to
midnight. About 150 FF.

An appetizing delicatessen and the Jewish restaurant par excellence in Paris. The specialities include pastrami, beef Stroganoff, tchoulent (Sabbath dish, with stuffed neck, buckwheat beans, stewing beef and beef marrow), stuffed carp or smoked salmon (homemade by the restaurant).

Mavrommatis

42, Rue Daubenton, 75005,
☎ 01.43.31.17.17.
M° Censier. To 11pm, closed
Mon. Menu 140 FF, à la carte
about 200-250 FF.

MAVROMMATIS
le restaurant

42 rue Daubenton - 75005 Paris
Réservation : 01 43 31 17 17

Arguably the best Greek restaurant in town. Settle comfortably into your sea-blue chair, and take your pick from thirty *mezze*, or first courses. Then try the shoulder of lamb with herbs, swordfish, mullet, or *sheftalia* (caul of lamb); the service is

charmingly and unmistakably Greek.

Le Square Trousseau

1, Rue Antoine Vollon 75012
Paris, ☎ 01.43.43.06.00.
M° Ledru-Rollin. Daily
noon-2:30pm, 8-11:30pm.

This restaurant is located next to a charming, typically Parisian garden not far from the Bastille. It has kept its original decor: mouldings on the ceiling, brown leather seats and an old bar with bevelled mirrors. The waiters wear long aprons, as they do in traditional brasseries. It's not surprising that this place is often used as a film set, and frequented by a trendy clientèle. The lunchtime menu is an excellent value at 135 francs, and includes tasty, imaginative dishes. Dinner, ordered à la carte, costs around 230 francs per person.

Polidor

41, Rue Monsieur-le-Prince,
75005, ☎ 01.43.26.95.34.
M° Luxembourg or Odéon.
To 12:30am. Menu 100 FF, à
la carte about 120 FF.

The decor is about 150 years old (notice the beautiful buffet where napkins are kept). It's crowded and friendly; the menu offers a hearty fare, including blanquette of veal and beef bourguignon. Don't miss the bathroom to see the wall-painting by César Auguste.

Brasserie des Musées

**49, Rue de Turenne, 75003,
☎ 01.42.72.96.17.
M° Saint-Paul. Daily 9am-
11pm; à la carte only.**

A traditional bistro in the heart
of the Marais, decorated in 1900s
style. Traditional cuisine, with
provincial dishes, including sausages with lentils, quiche, calf's
liver or sweetbread, and fish.
Main course: 65-90 francs.

Osteria del Passe-Partout

**20, Rue de l'Hirondelle,
75006, ☎ 01.46.34.14.54.
M° St-Michel. Closed Sun.
Menus 86, 94, 130 FF.**

It's a surprise to find a great
Italian restaurant so near Saint-
Michel. Enjoy the savoury rab-
bit and pasta, and the delicious
smells of basil and sage in a
warm, southern atmosphere.

Le Perron

**6, Rue Perronet, 75007,
☎ 01.45.44.71.51.
M° Saint-Germain-des-Prés.
Closed Sun. night, 200 FF.**

A Saint-Germain atmosphere
and southern Italian specialities: spaghetti with crayfish or
cuttlefish ink, tortellini with snails.
There's a wide range of starters,
and delicious homemade desserts. Reservations advised.

Le Bistro Mazarin

**42, Rue Mazarine, 75006,
☎ 01.43.29.99.01. M° Odéon.
Daily noon-4pm, 7:30 to
midnight; à la carte only.**

A classic bistro with paper tablecloths, and a young, trendy cliente-
tele of literati. If you go easy on
the wine, you can have a meal
for 130-150 francs, with a start-
er (hot goat's cheese salad, eggs
mimosa), and main course

(bourguignon, veal chop, steak
au bleu). It has a large selection
of Bordeaux wines. In fine
weather, relax on the terrace at
the corner of the Rue Callot.

Le Café des Lettres

**53, Rue de Verneuil, 75007,
☎ 01.42.22.52.17.
M° Rue du Bac.
To 11pm, closed Sun.
A la carte 150-200 FF.**

There's a relaxed, intellectual atmosphere in this Scandinavian
restaurant run by two Finnish
women. Smoked and marinated
fish specialities (herring, salmon) and fish croquettes. Seating on the patio in fine weather.

Thoumieux

**79, Rue Saint-Dominique,
75007.
☎ 01.47.05.49.75.
M° Latour-Maubourg.
Daily noon-3:30, 6:30pm to
midnight. Menu 82 FF.**

A large, classic brasserie, with
excellent homemade products
(specialities from the southwest,
such as foie gras). The service is
efficient, and many of the customers are regulars.

Virgin Café

**58-60, Champs-Élysées,
75008. ☎ 01.42.89.46.81.
M° George V or
Franklin- Roosevelt.
Daily to midnight.
A la carte: 100 FF; Sun.
brunch: 84 and 125 FF.**

A relaxed place, popular with
young people, for a drink (wine
by the glass) or for a good

dinner after exploring the music and video store. Happy hour is from 5 to 7pm.

Le Clown Bar

114, Rue Amelot, 75011,
☎ 01.43.55.87.35.
M° Filles du Calvaire.
noon-3pm, 7pm-1am; closed
Sun. in summer. About 75 FF.

Next to the Cirque d'Hiver, this is a sort of 1920s-style clown museum. It's usually very busy. Traditional cuisine includes hot sausage with lentils, oxtail, with a good selection of regional wines.

Lina's

Blvd des Italiens, 75009
☎ 01.42.46.02.06
Ave. de l'Opéra, 75009.
☎ 01.47.03.30.29.
To 6pm, closed Sun.

Join the rush to try the most fashionable sandwiches in Paris! (other locations: Rue Étienne-Marcel, Rue Marbeuf, St-Sulpice). Prawns, salmon, smoked ham.

L'Avenue

41, Ave. Montaigne, 75008,
☎ 01.40.70.14.91.
M° Franklin-Roosevelt.
Daily 8am-midnight. Menu
175 FF (dinner), à la carte
250-300 FF.

The interior decorator Jacques Grange has given this brasserie a new look, more in keeping with the neighbourhood of TV studios and fashion houses. Call in for a club sandwich (even in the afternoon), a "chef's suggestion", a seafood platter, or the house speciality: snail risotto.

Colette

213, Rue Saint-Honoré,
75001. ☎ 01.55.35.33.90.
M° Tuileries. Mon.-Sat.
10:30am-7:30pm.

A "water bar" in a Soho-style boutique, with 20 varieties of bottled water, and good dishes. Great for a light lunch when you're in the neighbourhood.

Chartier

7, Rue du Fg Montmartre,
75009, ☎ 01.47.70.86.29.
M° Rue Montmartre.
Daily 11am-3pm, 6-10pm.
About 80 FF.

More than 1,500 meals are served every day in this one-of-a-kind cafeteria, which has been going strong since it opened in 1896. The decor is pure 1900s, with a big clock and a glass roof. The cuisine is traditional; join the Thursday crowd if you're fond of pig's trotters!

A FEW SPECIAL PLACES

Be forewarned: the decor may outshine the food.

Le Grand Véfour

17, Rue de Beaujolais, 75001, ☎ 01.42.96.56.27. M° Palais-Royal.

Louis XVI-style carved wood trim, 19th-century paintings (under glass) inspired by Pompeian frescoes. The table where Victor Hugo used to sit, with its view of the Palais-Royal, is very much in demand.

La Tour d'Argent

15-17, Quai de la Tournelle 75005, ☎ 01.43.54.23.31. M° Maubert-Mutualité.

You'll have one of the most beautiful views of Paris from the bay

windows overlooking Notre-Dame and the Seine. You may not be able to afford to eat here (reservations advised), but at least you know it exists!

Drouant

18, Rue Gaillon, 75002, ☎ 01.42.65.15.16. M° Opéra. To midnight. Menu 230 FF, à la carte 400 FF.

It may always be crowded, but don't leave without a look at the beautiful banister!

Lipp

151, Blvd Saint-Germain, 75006, ☎ 01.45.48.53.91. M° Saint-Germain-des-Prés. To 2am. About 250 FF.

Lipp was created in 1880 and is still worth a visit, even though the sauerkraut is not as good as it used to be. Frequented on Friday nights by the literary crowd (you may catch sight of some TV personalities), celebrities and politicians.

Le Procope

13, Rue de l'Ancienne-Comédie, 75006, ☎ 01.40.46.79.00. M° Odéon. Daily to 1am.

The oldest restaurant in the capital.

Lapérouse

51, Quai des Grands-Augustins, 75006, ☎ 01.43.26.90.14. M° Saint-Michel. To 10:30pm.

Pure magic.

Le Train Bleu

Gare de Lyon, 20 Blvd Diderot, 75012. ☎01.43.43.09.06. M° Gare de Lyon. To 10pm.

Before you leave for Avignon or Marseille, explore this historic train station restaurant, a veritable museum of train travel, much loved by Colette and Jean Gabin. Journey back in time, but don't miss your train!

Lucas-Carton

9 Pl. de la Madeleine, 75008, ☎ 01.42.65.22.90. M° Madeleine. Closed Sat. lunch and Sun.

The cuisine of Alain Senderens, in a decor of light-coloured wood.

La Closerie des Lilas

171, Blvd du Montparnasse, 75006, ☎ 01.40.51.34.50. M° Port-Royal. Open daily.

A haunt of writers, past and present. Order a cocktail at the bar and soak up the atmosphere of literary Paris.

Maxim's

3, Rue Royale, 75008, ☎ 01.42.65.27.94. M° Concorde. To 10:30pm; closed Sun. and Mon.

A superb Art Nouveau decor, classified a historical monument in

1979. Admire the glass roof, which has some 180 decorative motifs, and the mirrors and wall paintings. Come more for the decor than the food.

Fermette Marbeuf

5, Rue Marbeuf, 75008. ☎ 01.53.23.08.00. M° Franklin-Roosevelt. Daily to 11:30pm.

For the fantastic decor in the Belle Époque room.

shopping in Paris

There's always something happening in Paris, and there's always somewhere to shop, especially when you can choose from 30,000 large and small stores.

OPENING HOURS FOR SHOPS

Usually 9.30-10am to 6.30-7pm (department stores stay open late once a week and on Sundays for a few weeks before Christmas). Chain stores such as Monoprix and Prisunic stay open till 9 or even 10pm (to midnight on the Champs-Élysées). The Drugstore on the Champs-Élysées is open 24 hours a day.

Boutiques may close for an hour or so at lunchtime, and many close altogether for one month in the summer, usually in August.

The small local grocery stores, generally run by North Africans, open early and don't close till 11 or 12pm. The prices tend to be higher than in a Monoprix, for example, but they are convenient and often the only place to buy provisions late at night.

Food stores (butchers, cheese merchants, greengrocers) usually close from 1pm to 3 or 4pm, as well as Sunday afternoons and Mondays, but bakers, tobacconists and chemists usually don't close at during lunch hours.

You can also buy clothes, records, books, perfumes, jewellery, gadgets and souvenirs all day long.

SHOPPING CENTRES

A number of shopping centres have opened over the last 20 years: the Carrousel du Louvre (in the Grand Louvre, entrance at 99, Rue de Rivoli, 75001; closed Tuesdays), the Forum des Halles (entrance at the Rue Pierre Lescot or the Rue Berger, 75001; closed Sundays), and the shopping centre on the Champs-Élysées (between the traffic circle and the Rue de Berri) all have cafés, restaurants, fashion boutiques, jewellers, gift shops, bookshops. Good for wet-weather days, but they're often crowded.

THE SHOPPER'S CAPITAL: A LONG-STANDING TRADITION

Early on, guilds of shopkeepers and craftsmen set up in specific areas of the town, a tradition which persists to this day. You'll find crystal and porcelain on the Rue de Paradis; bookshops and publishers in the vicinity of Saint-Germain-des-Prés and Odéon; furniture and hardware stores along Faubourg Saint-Antoine; musical instruments and sheet music on the Rue de Rome behind the Saint-Lazare station, and on the streets leading to the Place Pigalle. Avant-garde fashion designers are at (or near) the Place des Victoires, while the world's most famous jewellers are centred on the Rue de la Paix and the Place Vendôme.

The best place to purchase fabrics is at the Marché Saint-Pierre (at the foot of the Sacré-Coeur), and several computer stores are on the Avenue Daumesnil, near the Gare de Lyon train station.

PRICES

Prices must be marked by retailers and it's not customary to bargain in stores. But at flea markets, secondhand dealers and some antique dealers, haggling is the name of the game.

So you've found the night table of your dreams in one of the department stores? Before your dream becomes a nightmare, check on delivery procedures (if you paid over 1,000 francs and have an address near Paris, delivery is free); if you live in the provinces or abroad, delivery will cost extra, depending on the transport prices.

PAYING FOR YOUR PURCHASES

If you don't have cash, you can usually pay by Visa, which is the most widely accepted card in Paris; generally shops and restaurants also take American Express, Diner's Club or Eurocard (look for a sign on the door).

In theory, Eurocheques can be used in France, but few shops accept them. Banks will cash them, but may insist on a minimum amount. You can use them in the larger deparment stores, however.

If you don't want to keep too much cash on you, you can always go to one of the cash dispensers for occasional withdrawals; they're open 24 hours a day all over the capital (withdrawals up to 3,000 francs a week).

Although traveller's cheques are vaunted as safe and easy to use, French shopkeepers (and restaurants) often balk at accepting them, suggesting instead that you change them first at the nearest bank.

DELIVERY AND SHIPPING

If you find the little 19th-century dressing table or Charles X bed that you've always wanted, you can have the antique dealer or store send it on to you, or a private carrier (cost according to volume).

If you want your purchase sent abroad, it will have to be packed in a wooden crate, and the salesman will make out a proforma invoice for customs purposes.

CUSTOMS

If you take an antique (not regarded as part of France's cultural heritage, otherwise you need special permission from the French museum services) to another European Union country, you must pay all taxes and keep the invoice. In this case, you will have nothing to declare. For Americans and other non EU nationalities, buy exclusive of VAT: the shopkeeper will give you an export sales slip which will be stamped at customs when you leave France; you send a duplicate back to the store on arrival and he will recover the tax. If you have a solid silver canteen of cutlery in your travelling bag, keep the invoice with you (with details like hallmark, period and so on). Likewise for heavier items, transported by a carrier.

Customs information:
☎ 01.40.24.65.10.

QUINTESSENTIAL PARIS

There are certain "musts" on any shopping expedition in Paris; they are not necessarily chic or expensive, but they do reflect the best the capital has to offer. Here are a few suggestions to start with.

Guerlain

68, Ave. des Champs-Élysées, 75008.
☎ 01.45.62.52.57.
M° Franklin D. Roosevelt.
Daily 9:45am-7pm; closed Sun.

The most beautiful perfume shop in Paris. A decor dating from 1912, all marble and mirrors. In addition to the famous perfumes with their Proustian names, you will find a whole range of exclusive accessories, like brushes or combs (245 francs)

Benneton

75, Blvd Malesherbes 75008. ☎ 01.43. 87. 57. 39.
M° Saint-Augustin.
Mon-Fri. 9am-6:15pm, Sat. 9am-noon; closed Sun.

This long-standing Parisian family business, founded in 1880, is one of the few which still practises the craft of

engraving. It looks like a 19th-century chemist or a select English gentlemen's club, where customers are greeted as old friends. Distinguished stamped calling cards, with a gouache border, or a floral or animal design, cost 19 francs per card, with matching envelope, 180 francs for ten and 685 francs for 50. You can also order personalised cards.

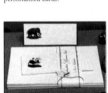

Angélina

226, Rue de Rivoli, 75001.
☎ 01.42.60.82.00.
M° Tuileries. Daily 9am-7pm, Sat. and Sun. 9am-7:30pm.

This tea room, with its old-fashioned decor, is the perfect place to relax after a visit to the Louvre or a walk through the Tuileries. Try the inimitable hot chocolate, famous all over

Paris. The dessert of choice is, of course, a Mont Blanc (a meringue and Chantilly cream covered with strands of chestnut cream) for 35 francs apiece. You can also buy chocolates here (360 francs/kilo).

Poilâne

8, Rue du Cherche-Midi, 75006.
☎ 01.45.48.42.59.
M° Sèvres-Babylone.
Daily 7:15am-8pm: closed Sun.

Parisians love Poilâne. This bakery, founded in 1936, is famous for its leavened bread, baked in a wood fire. It keeps for a week if wrapped up. A bread with a distinctive taste, delicious at breakfast, lunch or dinner. If you happen to live in France, you can have it sent to ryou doorstep and enjoy Poilâne toast for breakfast (81 francs for a 1-kilo loaf of bread, including delivery). Ask for a delivery form from one of the shopkeepers.

Androüet

41, Rue d'Amsterdam, 75008.
☎ 01.48.74.26.90.
M° Liège.
Daily 10am-2pm, 3-7:30pm; closed Mon. morning.

This ultra-famous store is a paradise for cheese connoisseurs, with 150 different varieties, from classics including the Camembert (27 francs) or Sainte-Maure (40 francs), to more unusual ones, such as Lou Picadou, which is a goat's cheese rolled in pepper. Delightful wooden gift-boxes make an original and appetising

gift: 160 francs for 6 cheeses, prepared to order, or 300 francs for 12.

Ladurée

16, Rue Royale, 75008.
☎ 01.42.60.21.79.
M° Madeleine.
Daily 8:30am-7pm,
Sun. 10am-7pm.

This refined and classy Parisian tea room is an institution. It's famous throughout the country, most of all for its speciality, macaroons. Coffee, chocolate, pistachio, vanilla: you'll find a flavour for every taste. Macaroons to take away cost 17 francs each, or 340 francs a kilo if you're

really greedy! They will keep 4 or 5 days in the refrigerator.

À la Mère de Famille

35, Rue du faubourg
Montmartre, 75009.
☎ 01.47.70.83.69.
M° Le Peletier.
Tues.Fri. 8:30am-1:30pm, 3-7pm; Sat. 8:30am-12:30pm, 3-7pm; closed Sun. and Mon.

Without doubt, one of the most beautiful stores in Paris. The atmosphere is turn-of-the-century, with ebony trim and blue-and-white tiling. The confectionery is traditional, from the French provinces (sugared almonds, shortbread cookies and madeleines). If you have a sweet tooth, you'll love the "délice de la mer": chocolate coated in rum-and-raisin flavoured almond paste (38 francs for 100gr). And to top it all, a fine selection of regional liquors (old armagnac 262 francs, calvados 173 francs).

La Civette

157, Rue Saint-Honoré, 75001.
☎ 01.42.96.04.99.
M° Palais-Royal-Musée du Louvre. Daily 9:30am-7pm; closed Sun.

A legendary address for Parisian smokers, with tobacco, pipes (some beauties), and all kinds of accessories, including the Humidor, a cigar box with a humidifier (1,100 francs). This store is also famous for its cigars from Cuba, Santo

SPECIAL MENTION:

Barthélémy, the other great Parisian cheese store (51, Rue de Grenelle, 75007, ☎ 01.42.22.82.24); **Berthillon,** THE Parisian ice-cream store, for inimitable sorbet (see p. 59); **Mariage Frères** for a selection of teas (see p. 108) ; **Hédiard,** for crystallized fruits (see p. 36); **Verlet** for coffee (see p. 109); **Lachaume** for cut flowers and bouquets (10, rue Royale, 75008, ☎ 01.42.60.57.26.); **Dalloyau,** for exceptional croissants at 5 francs apiece at the Place du Luxembourg from 8:30am on (2, Pl. Edmond Rostand, 75006, ☎ 01.43.29.31.10.).

Domingo or Honduras. From 13 to 130 francs each. A box of 25 starts at 450 francs.

WOMEN'S WEAR, HEAD TO TOE

Here's a look at the best in Paris fashion—daywear, evening dress, designs for town or country, workday or holiday. There's something for everyone and for (almost) every budget. Where to buy high heels or flats, minis or maxis, cottons or silks, party dresses or business suits—and huge hold-alls to carry home all your goods.

CLOTHES

Gap

14, Rue Lobineau, 75006.
☎ 01.44.32.07.30.
M° Odéon
or St.-Germain-des-Prés.
Mon.-Sat. 10am-8pm.

Straight from the States. New stock arrives every six weeks, and the previous collection is sold off. Jeans, basics, and sportswear. Shirts from 145 to 400 francs.

Schinichiro Arakawa

1, Rue du Plâtre, 75004.
☎ 01.42.78.24.21.
M° Hôtel de Ville.
Mon.-Sat. 11am-7:30pm.

This fantastic boutique is the perfect setting for the fashions designed by this up-and-coming Japanese creator. This is the only place in France where you can find the amazing Ian Reeds shoes or the photo magazine Zine 3. T-shirts for 230 francs, dresses 1,500 francs.

Loft

12, Rue du Faubourg Saint-Honoré, 75008.
☎ 01.42.65.59.65.
M° Madeleine.
56, Rue de Rennes, 75006.
☎ 01.45.44.88.99.
M° Saint-Germain-des-Prés.
Mon.-Sat. 10am-7pm.

A New York warehouse decor and reasonable prices. Sports shirts, shirts, T-shirts, all wrapped in cloth covers. The style is modern, natural. Stretch trousers, 750 francs; shirts, 380 francs.

Lolita Lempicka

2 bis, Rue des Rosiers, 75004.
☎ 01.42.74.50.48.
M° Saint-Paul.
Mon.-Sat. 10:30am-7pm.

Theatrical designs, crinolines on evening dresses, glamorous bodices. Slim-fitting suits and dresses with a touch of lace, a trace of see-through, a hint of pink. Evening dress for 3,350 francs.

Studio Lolita

2, Rue des Rosiers, 75004.
☎ 01.48.87.09.67. Tues.-Sun. 10:30am-1pm, 2-7pm.

The clothes here are from earlier collections.

CHEMICAL FABRICS

How well do you know artificial and synthetic fabrics? Artificial fabrics are constituted from a cellulose pulp, made from conifers or broad-leaved trees like beech or birch. Viscose, acetate or Modal are made in this way. Synthetic fabrics (polyamide, polyester, acrylic...) are made from a petroleum derivative known as naphtha. The chemical transformation of the raw material creates the strands which are made into thread, and then used to weave synthetic fabrics..

Clothes and colours straight from India, for those with a taste for far-off regions and styles. You'll find cashmeres, cotton chambray, cotton net in a range of warm Indian reds, yellows, oranges. The Nehru jacket is a popular design and the silk trousers are sublime (from 850 francs).

Être ronde en couleurs

1, Rue de Rivoli, 75004.
☎01.48.04.56.57.
M° St Paul.
Mon. 2:30-7pm,
Tues.-Sat.
10:30am-7pm.

The place to find all you need for the fuller figure, from lingerie to marvellous evening wear.

Doria Salambo

38, Rue de la Roquette, 75011.
☎ 01.47.00.06.30.
M° Bastille.
Mon. 2-8pm,
Tues.-Sat. 11am-8pm.

Doria creates her own styles and works her fabrics; she can also adapt them to your taste. Suits from 1,000 francs.

Sunshine

48 bis, Rue de Rivoli, 75004.
☎ 01.42.72.02.50.
M° Hôtel de Ville.
172, Rue du Temple, 75003.
Tél. 01 48 04 55 20.
M° Temple. Mon.-Sat. 9:30am-7:30pm.

All sorts of things at all sorts of prices: skirts for

200 francs, 70's style pants or hound's-tooth suits, and larger sizes too (up to 52).

Martin Grant

32, Rue des Rosiers, 75004.
☎ 01.42.71.39.49.
M° St Paul.
Tues.-Sun. 1-8pm.

Once a Jewish barbershop, now an Australian fashion house! This is the only place you'll find this superb crêpes de Chine and surprising gauzes. Dresses for 1,500 francs.

LINGERIE

Comme des Femmes

31, Rue St Placide, 75006.
☎01.45.48.97.33.
M° St Placide.
Mon.-Sat. 10am-7pm.

A Parisian soirée in inappropriate undies? Unthinkable! You'll find what you need here, at attractive prices. All the big name lingerie, for 30-50 per cent less than elsewhere. A wide range of tights in winter and swimsuits in summer.

Les Mariées de Lolita

15, Rue Pavée, 75004.
☎ 01.48.04.96.96.
Tues.-Sat. 10:30am-1:30pm,
2:30-7pm.

Marvellous fantasies in lace and taffeta.

Maria

28, Rue Pierre Lescot, 75001.
☎01.40.13.06.00.
M° Étienne Marcel.
Mon.-Sat. 10:30am-7:30pm.

Exclusive creations: superb backless dresses in tricot or tactel (just like a second skin) from 790 to 1,490 francs, and 30 tops that are really unique: some are straight and simple, others are crisscrossed with lace (200 to 400 francs).

Mohanjeet

21, Rue Saint-Sulpice, 75006.
☎ 01.43.54.73.29.
M° Odéon.
Mon. 2-7pm, Tues.-Sat.
10:30am-7pm.

BLOUSES

Big Ben Club

72, Rue Bonaparte, 75006.
☎ 01.40.46.02.12.
M° Saint-Sulpice.
Mon.-Sat. 10:30am-7pm.

This is the first shop in Paris which specialised in white blouses, and it's become an institution. Grass cloth, cotton piqué and pure cotton, with more than 80 styles from 295 to 395 francs, sizes 38 to 46.

Anne Fontaine

64, 66, Rue des Saints-Pères, 75007.
☎ 01.45.48.89.10.
M° Saint-Germain-des-Prés.
Mon.-Sat. 10am-7pm.
50, Rue Étienne-Marcel, 75002.
☎ 01.40.41.08.32.
M° Étienne Marcel.
Mon. 2-7pm,
Tues.-Sat. 10:30am-7pm.

Immaculate whites, cottons, poplins and organdies; special attention to detail with pretty buttons and cuffs; transparent vests to wear with or without the blouses. More than 60 styles from 350 to 750 francs.

BAGS AND ACCESSORIES

Swatch Store

10, Rue Royale, 75008.
☎ 01.42.60.58.38.
M° Concorde.
Mon.-Sat. 9:30am-7pm.

You'll find all the Swatch watches here, and much more besides! For an annual subscription of 500 francs, you can join the *Swatch Collector's* club, which entitles you to a collector's watch every year and a guide to all the previous designs. You'll also be given the secret code to access a Swatch swap service.

Totale Éclipse

40, Rue de la Roquette, 75011.
☎ 01.48.07.88.04.
M° Bastille.
Mon.-Sat.
11am-
7:30pm.

Molten glass, ceramics, and silver-plated jewellery in original and unusual designs. The more classic creations come in a range of four basic colours. Necklaces and rings from 65 francs, and some tempting bags.

Upla

17, Rue des Halles, 75001.
☎ 01.40.26.49.96.
M° Châtelet.
Mon.-Sat. 10:30am-7pm.

Everyone knows the plastic-coated canvas pouch-bag, with its practical pockets (from 610 to

2,000 francs). Now a range of shirts, sports jumpers and soft leather bags in four colours.

HATS

Axes et Soirs

97, Rue Vieille-du-Temple, 75003.
☎ 01.42.74.13.62.
M° Saint-Paul.
Mon.-Fri. 10am7pm,
Sat. 11am-7pm.

Two designers with loads of new ideas make these stylish, original hats. Made-to-order hats which cost almost the same as ready-to-wear, and they fit like a glove! You can bring your own fabric along too. About 1,000 francs each.

Marie Mercié

56, Rue Tiquetonne, 75002.
☎ 01.40.26.60.68.
M° Étienne Marcel.
23, Rue Saint-Sulpice, 75006. ☎ 01.43.26.45.83.
M° Odéon.
Mon.-Sat. 11am-7pm.

She works magic, blended with a touch of poetry and humour. She's as clever with straw as she is with velvet, and you may come away wearing a bird on your head, or an admiral's hat! Two collections a year, hats from 650 francs and up.

SOCKS AND TIGHTS

Bleu-Forêt

33, Rue des Petits-Champs, 75002.
☎ **01.40.20.00.17.**
M° Palais-Royal-Musée du Louvre.
Mon.-Fri. 10am-7pm,
Sat. 11am-6pm.
59, Rue de Rennes, 75006.
☎ **01.45.48.27.46.**
M° Saint-Sulpice.
Tues.-Sat. 10am-7:30pm.

Cotton, linen, yarn, wool, chiné, plain, flowered. These socks are made for showing off! Classic and sporty tights, and women's knee socks. From 55 francs.

SHOES

Mosquitos

25, Rue du Four, 75006.
☎ **01.43.25.25.16.**
M° Mabillon.
Mon.-Sat.
10am-7:30pm.
19, Rue Pierre Lescot, 75001.
☎ **01.45.08.44.72.**
M° Les Halles.
Mon.-Sat.
10:30am-7:30pm.

What's biting you? Cheer yourself up with these original shoes, stitched together with a multitude of colours; from 195 to 1,500 francs.

Free Lance

22, Rue Mondétour, 75001.
☎ **01.42.33.74.70.**
M° Les Halles
or Étienne-Marcel.
Mon.-Fri. 10am-7pm,
Sat. 10am-7:30pm.

Always in tune with the current fashion, or whatever's back in style. Classics and originals, flats and heels. For ages 20 to 50. Trainers from 280 to 400 francs, shoes from 1,000 francs, boots around 1,500 francs.

Camper

25, Rue du Vieux-Colombier, 75006.
☎ **01.45.48.22.00.**
M° Saint-Sulpice.
Mon.-Sat. 10am-7pm.

The left shoe and right shoe aren't the same? That's Camper! The Mix collection is urban-techno and made of futuristic materials (nylons and

leathers).
The *Cartujana de Espana* is another Camper design. Ultra-comfortable, nice colours, prices around 550 francs.

MEN'S WEAR, TOP TO TOE

Whether you're a classic or eccentric, nature-lover, businessman, cyber-freak, or strictly a city person, in just one weekend you can redo your entire wardrobe. Wild hats, smart ties, handmade shoes, embroidered waistcoats, chequered shirts, original jackets from England, Italy, America, France, you've got a world of fashion at your feet.

Lionel Nath

7, Rue Béranger, 75003.
☎ 01.48.87.81.30.
M° République.
Mon.-Sat. 9am-6:30pm.

Direct sales from a designer-manufacturer whose prices haven't gone up in the last 5 years. Fine quality, wide choice

of pure wool suits for 1,000 francs, super-100 wool for 1,400 francs. Summer jackets in microfibre for 700 francs, pure cashmere winter ones for 1,000 francs.

Anthony Peto

12, Rue Jean-Jacques Rousseau, 75001.
☎ 01.42.21.47.15.
M° Palais-Royal-Musée du Louvre.
Mon.-Sat. 11am-7pm.

If you feel you must have a snakeskin beret or a black fez with a red pompon, this is definitely the place for you! And if you prefer a bowler, Panama or cap, you'll still be spoilt for choice. Fedoras start at 600 francs; top hats for 980 francs and up.

Brummell

61, Rue Caumartin, 75009.
☎ 01 42 82 50 00. M° Havre-Caumartin. Mon.-Sat. 9:30am-7pm, Thurs. to 10pm.

Part of the Printemps department store is named after the famous English dandy. A men's wear shop with all the major names and styles: classic, sportswear and more unusual clothes, from underwear in the basement to suits on the fourth floor. The "Brummell" collection comes

out twice a year, and offers elegant clothes at a reasonable price.

Smuggler

Village Royal,
25, Rue Royale, 75008.
☎ 01.42.66.01.31.
M° Madeleine.
64, Rue Bonaparte, 75006.
☎ 01.46.34.72.29.
M° Saint-Sulpice.
Mon. 2-7:30pm,
Tues.-Sat.
10:30am-1pm,
2-7:30pm
(7:15pm
Village
Royal).

With more than 400 fabrics, Smuggler is a specialist in made-to-order suits which cost just about the same as the ones in the ready-to-wear collection. Anything goes: Mao collars, original buttons, trousers with or without pleats. Custom-made clothes take two weeks. 1,960 francs for a super 100 wool suit. And this is the place to find the cheapest Alden shoes in Paris.

Le Shop

3, Rue d'Argout, 75002.
☎ 01.40.28.95.94.
M° Étienne Marcel.
Mon.-Sat. 11am-7pm.

The theme is "world culture", the makes are many and various. New styles to go with techno music, house, rap and acid jazz.

Shoes and jackets, T-shirts and dungarees. Northwave-sample shoes, Airwork trainers, a bar-brasserie for a quick snack and Internet as well. You'll also find secondhand clothes and bikes. Trousers from 285 to 600 francs, shirts from 250 to 500 francs.

Blundstone boots (690 francs) and Trippen clogs (490 to 640 francs). Suggested attire: try the restyled turn-of-the-century work clothes, especially the Largeot trousers.

Sagone
44-46, Ave. de la République, 75011.
☎ 01.49.29.92.83.
M° Parmentier.
Mon.-Sat. 10am-7:30pm.

Latino Rock
15, Rue de la Grande Truanderie, 75001.
☎ 01.45.08.17.01.
M° Les Halles.
Mon. noon-7:30pm, Tues.-Sat. 11am-7:30pm.

Young or not-so-young, you'll love the reefer jackets (1,200 francs); or why not try a PVC one (799 francs) for a change of style? Tight-fitting T-shirts or satin shirts to wear with all kinds of suits (from 1,400 to 2,200 francs), and beautiful Jourdan Bis shoes.

SHOES

Anatomica
14, Rue du Bourg-Tibourg, 75004.
☎ 01.42.74.10.20.
M° St Paul-le-Marais.
Mon.-Sat. 10m30am-7:30pm, Sun.3-7:30pm.

"Shoes the shape of your feet" and authentic styles. Here you'll find the widest selection of Birkenstock shoes in France (from 320 to 550 francs), plus Australian

Timberland
52, Rue Croix-des-Petits-Champs, 75001.
☎ 01.45.08.41.40.
M° Palais-Royal.
Mon.-Sat. 10:30-7pm.

Shoes and clothes made of waterproof leather, specially designed for the outdoor life. They're made of natural fabrics like linen and cotton, in the warm orange, russet and brown colours of the Canadian forests. Timberland was the first to make round-toed boots with padded ankles, then everyone copied them. From 1,100 francs a pair. Shirts from 450 francs.

If you have a hard time finding shoes for extra-large feet, try this shop, which stocks sizes from 39 to 50. Shoes to go out in, to go walking in, to get married in! From 400 to 1,500 francs. And if your wife wears from size 33 to 44, bring her along too.

Fenestrier

23, Rue du Cherche-Midi,
75006.
☎ 01.42.22.66.02.
M° Saint-Sulpice.
Mon.-Fri. 10am-12:30pm, 2-
7pm; Sat. 10am-7pm.

Dark brown is one of the favourite
colours here. The designs are
classic, with a younger line
of two-tone leather and canvas
shoes with rubber soles. The
summer speciality is canvas shoes
and sandals. Handmade, from
800 francs.

TIES

Cravatterie
Nazionali

249, Rue Saint-Honoré,
75001.
☎ 01.42.61.50.39.
M° Concorde or Madeleine.
Mon.-Sat. 10am-7pm.

This shop has an impressive
selection of some 5,000 ties,
with about 20 makes, and silk
Cravatterie ties from 245 francs
and up. Six hundred styles
rolled in pairs in wooden cabinets;
you're free to explore through
the drawers and take your pick.

Jean-Charles
de Castelbajac

6, Pl. Saint-Sulpice, 75006.
☎ 01.46.33.87.32.
M° Saint-Sulpice.
Mon.-Sat. 10am-7pm.

Castelbajac likes fun ties,
especially silk ones with woven
and relief patterns. Moons,
suns, stars and hearts are the
designer's favourite motifs.
You'll find reds and yellows, lovely
beiges and greys, as well as
beautiful navys. From 400 francs.

SHIRTS

Le Fou du Roi

55-57, Rue de Vaugirard,
75006.
☎ 01.45.44.07.82.
M° Rennes.
Mon.-Sat. 10am-7:30pm.

To brighten up your days or stand
out in a crowd, choose your
shirts here. They're multicoloured
and well-cut; a poplin shirt costs
250 francs, and you'll also find
silk and linen ones (very
comfortable for the summer).
Beautiful silk ties (150 or
230 francs) and silk waistcoats
(390 francs). Superb suits (cupro,
linen, viscose, velvet or
microfibre), from 1,250 to
2,250 francs.

Bain Plus

51, Rue des
Francs-
Bourgeois, 75004.
☎ 01.48.87.83.07.
M° Saint-Paul.
Tues.-Sat. 11am-
7:30pm;
Sun 2-7pm.

Herringbone shirts, so soft
you want to sleep in them;
flannelette for winter,
and seersucker poplin
for summer. An exclusive
handmade collection
of pyjamas (from
550 francs and up),
shorts (starting at

130 francs) and dressing gowns.
You can also pick up matching
mules and toilet bags.

WAISTCOATS

Favour Brook

Le Village Royal,
25, Rue Royale, 75008.
☎ 01.40.17.06.72.
M° Madeleine.
Mon.-Sat. 10am-7pm.

Waistcoats made by an English tailor. The style is 18th-century dandy, with a touch of English eccentricity. Cotton and printed velvet brocades, silk embroidery. Some 300 ready-to-wear waistcoats, and 2,000 fabrics for made-to-order (from 1,100 to 2,100 francs). Jackets with Nehru collars for 4,000 francs, tail coats and morning coats from 4,500 to 5,000 francs. There's a new ladies' collection, with various styles of jacket, and dresses for 3,000 francs. An up-and-coming boutique.

LEATHER

Michel Lipsic

52, Rue Croix-des-Petits-Champs, 75001.
☎ 01.40.41.97.47.
M° Palais-Royal-Musée du Louvre.
Mon.-Sat. 10:30am-7pm.

Attractive pale-blue or apple-green shirts in machine or handwashable Indian mixed leather. The great classics: the safari jacket Clark Gable wore in *Mogambo*, Marlon Brando's jacket in *On the Waterfront*. Made-to-order clothes for the same price as ready-to-wear, an on-the-spot workshop for alterations, more than ten qualities of leather and a vast range of colours. Trousers from 1,900 francs.

Le carreau du temple

Rue Dupetit-Thouars and
Rue Perrée, 75003.
M° Temple. Tues.-Sat. 9am-12:30pm; Sun and holidays 9am-1pm.

Impecunious Parisians have been shopping for clothes under this glass roof for over 200 years, and even if the prices have changed, the tradition of bargaining hasn't! It's something to remember when you find the leather jacket of your dreams (there's a wide selection, with prices from 800 to 1,000 francs). There are also specialist stores worth a visit in the Rue Dupetit-Thouars.

CHILDREN'S CLOTHES AND TOYS

Paris has something for every kind of child (and parent or grandparent, for that matter): cute little smocked dresses and bloomers for the princess look, casual T-shirts and jumpers for easy wear, and stretch jeans and jackets. Plenty of fashions to choose from and plenty of gift-ideas for your little darlings, be they darlings or devils.

La Cerise sur le Gâteau

82, Rue de la Victoire, 75009. ☎ 01.44.53.98.89. M° Chaussée d'Antin. Mon.-Fri. 10am-7pm; Sat. 11am-7pm.

Classic or original designs, superb fabrics, clever cuts, and the cherry on the cake: reversible summer or winter outfits. Girls' dresses (0 to 16 years old) from 100 to 200 francs, boys' trousers (up to age 12) from 80 francs.

Chattawak

5, Rue Vavin, 75006. ☎ 01.40.46.85.64. M° Vavin. Mon.-Sat. 10am-7pm.

All kinds of clothes for boys and girls. A chic sportswear collection in blue, white and red. Soft-on-the-skin cottons, comfortable fabrics, but hard-wearing and resistant too. Sweatshirts for 185 francs, lycra jeans 326 francs.

Lara et les Garçons

60, Rue Saint-Placide, 75006. ☎ 01.45.44.01.89. M° Saint-Placide. Tues.-Sat. 10am-7pm; Mon. noon-7pm.

A constant supply of designer seconds (clothes and shoes) for kids from 0 to 16. Lots of pretty dresses from 89 francs, trousers starting from 59 francs.

Osh Kosh B'Gosh

32, Rue de Passy, 75016. ☎ 01.46.12.09.70. M° Passy. Mon.-Sat. 10:30am-7pm.

An all-time American favourite since 1895. Osh-Kosh dungarees shipped direct from Wisconsin to Paris for kids from 3 months to 12 years old. A comfortable sportswear collection in ultra-resistant fabrics, USA-style. Junior dungarees start at 285 francs. And the store itself is worth a visit.

Si Tu Veux

68, Galerie Vivienne, 75002. ☎ 01.42.60.59.97. M° Bourse. Mon.-Sat. 10am-7pm.

Here's a store full of imagination and creativity, and a place to find intelligent gifts for your kids. Nearly everything comes in kit form: costumes to sew (from 120 to 200 francs) or ready-made (from 250 to 300 francs); party kits (with various themes: ghosts, the circus, and so); handiwork and kits for little chefs.

CROISSANT

3, Rue St Merri, 75004.
☎ 01.48.87.32.88.
M° Hôtel-de-Ville.
Mon.-Sat. 11am-1:30pm,
2:30-7pm.

It's like being in a doll's house, where everything looks good enough to eat! Croissant has been making its own designs for 20 years, and has built up a faithful clientele. The shelves are full of handmade baby clothes (so who cares if you can't knit?) A good selection of clothes for older children, too (up to 8 years old).

Jeux Descartes

52, Rue des Écoles, 75005.
☎ 01.43.26.79.83.
M° Cluny-La Sorbonne.
Mon. 11am-7pm;
Tues.-Sat. 10am-7pm.

Everything that gets your brain ticking: puzzles, role-playing games (prices from 50 to 500 francs), games of strategy.

Tarots and card games from all over the world, including billiards and backgammon, plus a large selection of model soldiers.

Multicubes

5, Rue de Rivoli, 75004.
☎ 01.42.77.10.77.
M° Saint-Paul.
Tues.-Sat. 10am-7pm.

Natural or painted wood. Puppets and spinning tops, cubes and puzzles, parlour games. All kinds of lovely objects for a child's bedroom, from night-lights to coat racks. Multicubes is also one of the few places where you'll find Steiff cuddly toys. About 100 francs for a puppet, and 200 francs for a height measuring tape.

Bazar

Royal Rivoli, 78 Rue de Rivoli, ☎ 01.42.72.68.79.
M° Hôtel de Ville. Lun.-sam. 9am-7:30pm.

A real bazar! Cuddly toys (from 25 francs) for tiny tots, puzzles (30 francs) for big brothers and sisters.

Bonpoint

86, Rue de l'Université, 75007.
☎ 01.45.51.46.28.
M° Solférino.
Mon.-Sat. 10am-7pm.
(see p. 45).

Score Games

56, Blvd Saint-Michel, 75006. ☎ 01.43.25.85.55.
M° Cluny-La Sorbonne.
Mon. noon-7pm; Tues.-Sat. 10am-7pm. 46, rue des Fossés-Saint-Bernard, 75005.** ☎ 01.43.29.02.90.
M° Jussieu.
Mon.-Sat. 10am-7pm.

The Parisian super-specialist in video games. More than 50,000 models for all consoles. New and secondhand, discounts of 30 to 80 per cent on certain products. All games can be returned, refunded or exchanged. There is also a PC and CDROM department. For more information: Minitel 3615 Score Games.

INTERIOR DECORATION

Everything you need to decorate and furnish your nest from top to bottom. Habitat was a pioneer more than 20 years ago; now there are plenty of stores where you can find great ideas, from pretty plates to designer beds. Just walking round the stores is a treat in itself! You're sure to come away with plans for transforming your home.

Globe Trotter

5, Rue de Médicis, 75006.
☎ 01.43.26.28.66.
M° Odéon.
Tues.-Sat. 11am-7pm.

Just opposite the Luxembourg Gardens. It looks like a secondhand store, with items out on the sidewalk for you to discover.

Coloured furniture reminiscent of southern France, with glazed pedestal tables to wrought-iron bud vases. Exclusive and original handcrafted designs. Glass and wrought-iron vases start from 230 francs. You can consult their catalogue for mail orders.

Avant-Scène

4, Pl. de l'Odéon, 75006.
☎ 01.46.33.12.40.
M° Odéon.
Tues.-Sat. 10:30am-1pm, 2-7pm.

Where decoration means innovation (see p. 48).

Conceptua

9, Rue de la Roquette, 75011.
☎ 01.43.38.68.87.
M° Bastille.
Mon.-Sat. 10am-7:30pm; Sun. 2-7:30pm.

This large store is a gold mine, with plenty of original items at affordable prices. Wrought-iron mirrors for 249 francs, sofa beds from 1,190 francs, contemporary-style valets for 495 francs, lamps for 249 francs, ready-made drapes for 395 francs. Plus, a "Colonial secondhand market" with mahogany and teak furniture, with some unusual pieces (folding chairs for 490 francs).

Despalles

Village Royal, 26, Rue Boissy-d'Anglas,75008.
☎ 01.49.24.05.65.
M° Madeleine.
Mon.-Sat. 10am-7pm, (see p. 36).

Maison de Famille

29, Rue Saint-Sulpice, 75006.
☎ 01.40.46.97.47.
M° Saint-Sulpice or Odéon.
Mon.-Sat. 10:30am-7pm.

Linen, crockery, glassware and gift ideas (see p. 48).

AGNÈS COMAR

7, Ave. George-V, 75008.
☎ **01.49.52.01.89.**
M° Alma-Marceau.
Tues.-Sat. 10:30am-1pm,
2-7pm; Mon. 2-7pm.

A marvelous store, with a charm all its own. Sophisticated and refined objects include silk, linen and organdy for the living room, dining room and bedroom. An abundance of ideas and a variety of materials for gifts at reasonable prices, if you can bear to give them away! Silk sheets in a mini-pouch for 190 francs; shantung cushions filled with potpourri for 320 francs; linen tablecloths for 780 francs.

Le Cèdre Rouge Côté Maison

25, Rue Duphot, 75008.
☎ **01.42.61.81.81.**
M° Madeleine.
Mon. noon-7pm; Tues.-Sat 10am-7pm.

Cèdre Rouge is aglow with warm, sunset colours of honey, raspberry, and olive. Real craftsmanship, with wrought iron, ceramic and rattan. Beautiful crockery, dazzling sofas, ultra-soft household linen. A very southern French collection. Ceramic salad-bowl, 125 francs; wrought-iron

chair, 850 francs. Mail-order service.

The Conran Shop

117, Rue du Bac, 75007.
☎ **01.42.84.10.01.**
M° Sèvres-Babylone.
Mon. noon-7pm; Tues.-Sat. 10am-7pm.

Just next to the Bon Marché department store, this shop is a haven of charm, simplicity and decorative genius, signed by Terence Conran, the creator of Habitat. The ultimate lifestyle store, where every object is a delight (for the eyes, if not for the purse): furniture—some of it exclusive—rugs, fabrics, crockery and lights. Glassware from 9 to 155 francs; plates from 16 to 170 francs; vases from 70 francs to 2,000 francs for a designer's vase in crystal. Admire the window displays, even if you don't go in.

Mis en Demeure

27, Rue du Cherche-Midi, 75006.
☎ **01.45.48.83.35.**
M° Sèvres-Babylone.
Mon. 1-7:30pm;
Tues.-Sat. 10am-7:30pm.

A modern store, despite the

nostalgia of its old-fashioned furniture and objects. Objects for the kitchen and bedroom, in soft colours and smelling of wax polish. Turned wood, cut glass, embroidered cushions, along with printed cotton tablemats for 95 francs; extending table with an old-fashioned sheen, 5,800 francs.

Contrepoint

59, Rue de Seine, 75006.
☎ **01.40.51.88.98.**
M° Mabillon.
Tues.-Sat. 10am-7pm.
62, Rue Jean-Jacques Rousseau, 75001.
☎ **01.40.26.56.95.**
M° Les Halles.
Mon. 2-7pm.

Bright and cheerful, with an intelligent, colourful mail-order catalogue. A fresh perspective on home decoration from a one-time fabric creator who's turned his hand to interior design, with drapes, rugs, cushions and headboards. Very comfortable armchairs and sofas, pretty crockery, pottery and lampshades. Items made-to-order, professional advice. Fabrics from 195 to 490 francs the metre; custom-made drapes from 475 francs.

THE ART OF TABLEWARE

The latest designs on exhibit in magnificent window displays; prestigious addresses, and neighbourhoods where all the shops are selling lovely tableware. New collections, which appear twice a year, present original designs and modern versions of classic favourites. Crockery for day-to-day use, special dishes for special occasions, festive touches for parties.

Bodum invented the piston-operated cafetière and teapot. Most of the items in the collection are simple and practical, wooden Danish designs. Pepper and salt mills, nutcrackers, breadboards, bottle racks, distinctive glass and wooden jars. Teapots from 115 to 180 francs.

Dîners en Ville
27, Rue de Varenne, 75007.
☎ **01.42.22.78.33.**
M° Rue du Bac.
Mon. 2-7pm; Tues.-Sat. 11am-7pm.

There are bright colours everywhere in this store, with printed tablecloths by Gérard Danton and Beauvillé, and French

Jacquard. Portuguese plates, crockery with raised decorative patterns. Cutlery with multi-coloured, mother-of-pearl or transparent handles (from 130 francs per item). Glasses from 60 to 200 francs each.

Kitchen Bazar
11, Ave du Maine, 75014.
☎ **01.42.22.91.17.**
M° Montparnasse-Bienvenüe.
Galerie des Trois Quartiers, 23, Blvd de la Madeleine, 75001. ☎ **01.42.60.50.30.**
M°Madeleine.
Mon.-Sat. 10am-7pm.

For 30 years, Kitchen Bazar has created new designs using contemporary materials, especially stainless steel. Kitchen utensils as beautiful as they are intelligent, made in the USA or in Japan, and meant to be seen. Stainless-steel toaster: 395 francs.

Laure Japy
36, Rue lu Bac, 75007.
☎ **01.42.86.96.97.**
M° Rue du Bac.
Mon.-Sat. 10:30am-2pm, 3-7pm.

Everything here is made to mix and match, including the Limoges china services. There are two

Bodum
99, Rue de Rivoli, Carrousel du Louvre, 3, Allée de Rivoli, 75001. ☎ **01.42.60.47.11.**
M° Palais-Royal-Musée du Louvre.
Daily 11am-8pm; Tues. noon-8pm.

collections a year, with new styles, patterns and colours. Glassware, coloured cutlery, tablecloths, undercloths and tablemats. Plates from 160 francs.

À la Mine d'Argent

108, Rue du Bac, 75007.
☎ 01.45.48.70.68.
M° Rue du Bac.
Mon.-Fri.
10am-
7pm,
Sat. 11am-6pm.

The is the ideal shop for antique silverware, both silver plate and solid silver, and you can buy one item or a whole set. This silver shop is a true gold mine when you're looking for the odd item of cutlery. There's a silversmith on the spot, who makes classic designs for reasonable prices. You can bring

in silver for all kinds of repairs, including silver-plating, embossment, engraving. 720 francs for a bread basket.

La Tisanière

21, Rue de Paradis, 75010.
☎ 01.47.70.22.80.
M° Poissonnière.
Mon.-Sat. 10am-6:30pm.

Lots of white china crockery you can decorate yourself, if you prefer the personal touch (plates for 20 francs and up). If your taste runs more towards traditional designs, you'll find copies of famous French 18th-century porcelain (plates from 65 francs). Glassware and cutlery too.

Diva

97, Rue du Bac, 75007.
☎ 01.45.48.95.39.
M° Rue du Bac.
Mon. 2-7pm;
Tues.-Sat. 11am-7pm.

Lights and objects made by master glass blowers from the island of Murano in Italy. Florentine glasses, in deep, warm Italian colours, including blues, greens, pinks, ambers and yellows. Dishes, salad bowls, vases, all shaped in Florentine glass. Glasses from 80 francs each.

La Chaise Longue

20, Rue des Francs-Bourgeois, 75003.
☎ 01.48.04.36.37.
M° Saint-Paul.
Mon.-Sat. 11am-7pm;
Sun. 2am-7pm.
8, Rue Princesse, 75006.
Closed Sun.
☎ 01.43.29.62.39.
M° Mabillon.
30, Rue Croix-des-Petits-Champs, 75001.
☎ 01.42.96.32.14. Closed
Sun. M°Louvre-Rivoli.

A lovely, unpretentious collection, with enamelled iron crockery in bright colours decorated with exotic flowers or Chinese fish. You can also find two-tone glasses and huge plates which can be used as trays. Enamelled plates for 40 francs and 45 francs.

EARTHENWARE OR BISCUITWARE?

■ **Ceramic:** Any pottery which has become hard through firing.

■ **Earthenware:** Ordinary (enamel-coated) or china (white paste with transparent glaze). There are famous factories in Rouen, Lille, Moustier, Gien, Nevers and Quimper.

■ **Porcelain:** This is created by the vitrification of the kaolin at around 2500° F. It is white, impermeable and translucent. Famous factories: Chantilly, Sceaux, Rouen, Limoges, Sèvres and Vincennes.

■ **Biscuitware:** White porcelain which has been fired several times but not glazed. It looks something like white marble. Biscuit is used more for figurines and ornaments than for crockery.

Gien

18, Rue de l'Arcade, 75008.
☎ **01.49.24.07.77.**
M° Madeleine.
Tues.-Sat. 10am-7pm.

Patterned pieces from the Gien
earthenware factory, for
use at breakfast,
lunch and
dinner.
A contemporary
line created by young
designers, featuring
floral patterns and
fresh colours. You can
personalise your plates
by adding your initials or
coat of arms. Prices start
at 395 francs for a set
of dessert plates.
Collector's items
can be ordered by
mail from the catalogue.

RUE ROYALE

What a fitting name for this
street, which is full of
prestigious stores specialising
in the art of tableware (crystal,
porcelain and more).
From Concorde to the
Madeleine, you can admire
the window displays of
Christofle, Ercuis, St-Hilaire,
Cocquet and Lalique, and
Bernardaud (tea room from
n° 9 to 21). Not to mention
Villeroy et Boch, Baccarat,
and Saint-Louis crystalware.

Simon

**36, Rue Étienne-Marcel,
75002.**
☎ **01.42.33.71.65.**
M° Les Halles.
Mon.-Sat. 8:30am-6:30pm.

White crockery for hotels and
English porcelain. The collections
of plates, dishes and glasses
(with nearly 15,000 different
items) are piled up in a most
professional way. Most
professional caterers and hotel
suppliers swear by this store.
You can restore your silver cutlery
here (35 francs per item).
An indispensable address for cooks
and gourmets.

Jean-Pierre de Castro

**17, Rue des
Francs-Bourgeois,
75004.**
☎ **01.42.72.04 00.**
M° Saint-Paul.
**Tues.-Fri. 10:30am-1pm,
2-7pm; Sat. 10am-7pm;
Sun. 11am-1pm, 2-7pm.**

All kinds of silverware (see
p. 62).

Kitchen Bazaar Autrement

**6, Ave du Maine,
75014.**
☎ **01.45.48.89.00.**
**M° Montparnasse-
Bienvenüe.**
Mon.-Sat. 10am-7pm.

Kitchen and tableware with an
exotic touch. Wood, terracotta,
glazed earthenware and
wickerwork in warm colours and
shapes inspired by craftsmen
from all over the world. Glazed
earthenware salad bowl from
58 francs.

Dehillerin

**18, Rue Coquillière,
75001.**
☎ **01.42.36.53.13.**
**M° Louvre-Rivoli
or Étienne Marcel.**
**Mon. 8am-12:30pm, 2-6pm;
Tues.-Sat. 8am-6pm.**

Everything for the kitchen (see p. 56).

La Maison Ivre

38, Rue Jacob,
75006.
☎ 01.42.60.01.85.
M° Saint-Germain-des-Prés.
Tues-Sat. 10:30am-7pm.

The crockery here is all handcrafted, in the blues, honey-colours and greens of Provence. Original patterns and a selection of printed tablecloths with fruit-and-flower designs, which goes well with the natural designs of the pottery. Decorated plates from 135 francs, plain plates from 75 francs.

Quartz

12, Rue des Quatre-Vents, 75006.
☎ 01.43.54.03.00.
M° Odéon.
Mon. 14:30am-7pm;
Tues.-Sat.
10:30am-7pm.

The ultimate glassware store. From artists' original designs to the simplest of glasses, with exclusive signed pieces and everyday objects. Decanters, plates and vases, candleholders and cheese covers. Dishes and salad bowls in red, green, blue or amber. "Classics" like the ringed decanter (150 francs), or the square "Zen" plate (280 francs).

Siècle

24, Rue du Bac,
75007.
☎ 01.47.03.48.03.
M° Rue du Bac.
Mon.-Sat. 10:30am-7pm.
(see p. 45).

Boutique Paris Musées

Forum des Halles,
1, Rue Pierre Lescot,
75001.
☎ 01.40.26.56.65.
M° Les Halles.
Tues.-Sat. 10:30am-7pm;
Mon. 2-7pm.

Items by contemporary designers who are inspired by the Paris museums or who dream up their own designs; a selection of tableware for everyday use or for special occasions. The Gien "Majolica" service, pieces from 60 to 400 francs; the "Faitoo" series by Philippe Starck, from 35 to 500 francs.

Taïr Mercier

7, Blvd Saint-Germain,
75005.
☎ 01.43.54.19.97.
M° Maubert-Mutualité.
Tues.-Fri. 11am-7pm;
Sat. 2:30-7pm.

A complete set of Taïr Mercier plastic-coated tablemats, to make every meal a party (from 25 to 65 francs). Exclusive designs for plates (from 25 francs), glasses (from 10 francs), cutlery and even paper serviettes. Some articles are unique. Handmade plates from 120 francs.

WHAT'S NEW?

You can be sure that journalists, designers and decorators know all these addresses. The furniture and accessories in these stores are often signed by the designers, and they are sometimes made in limited series only. Love them or hate them, but you won't be indifferent. Who knows, perhaps the piece you choose today will become a model of contemporary design. Even if you don't buy, at least go and take a look.

Some 150 young designers exhibit together just next to Beaubourg; jewellery, T-shirts, lamps, hundreds of bits and pieces in plastic, paper, recycled wood. Exclusive items at affordable prices. Jewellery from 50 to 800 francs. Gift ideas for all tastes.

Artistes et Modèles

3, Rue Jacques-Callot, 75006.
☎ 01.46.33.83.20.
M° Odéon.
Tues.-Sat. 11am-1pm, 2:30am-7pm.

A little store in the Beaux-Arts neighbourhood. You'll find a reproduction of the chrome and leather armchair (1927) by Mies van der Rohe, and the genuine Thonet seat which featured in all of Le Corbusier's interiors. There are contemporary designs too, like the Ron Arad bookcase, the Philippe Starck ashtray and dadada stool, plus works by Charlotte Maugirard. Vases by Gaetano Pesce from 360 francs.

Avant-Musées

2, Rue Brisemiche, 75004.
☎ 01.48.87.45.81.
M° Rambuteau.
Mon.-Fri. noon-7pm;
Sat. 1-7pm.

Astier de Villatte

105, Ave. Daumesnil, 75012. ☎ 01.43.45.72.72.
M° Bastille or Gare de Lyon.
Mon.-Sat. 11am-7pm.

An artful mix of the modern and the traditional in this collection that recalls period furniture, although with a few original touches. Enamelled terracotta from a Parisian workshop: vases, bowls and crockery. Everything is handmade; choose from a wide range of colours. Plates from 160 francs, vases from 540 francs.

Via

Viaduc des Arts, 29-37 Ave. Daumesnil, 75012.
☎ 01.46.28.11.11.
M° Gare de Lyon or Bastille.
Mon.-Fri. 10am-7pm.

Not just a store but a gallery where you can see the latest trends in the French furnishings industry, with a thematic exhibition every six weeks. The place is a monument in itself, located under the arches of an old viaduct. The whole district is being renovated, the arcades are filling up with boutiques and workshops, and the old railway has been replaced by a

new terraced garden, the *coulée verte* (green trail), which goes almost all the way to the Parc de Vincennes.

Jean-Charles de Castelbajac

6, Pl. Saint-Sulpice, 75006.
☎ 01.46.33.87.32.
M° Saint-Sulpice.
Mon.-Sat. 10am-7pm.

He can make a coat from a rug, or reversible couch-covers which look good enough to wear! His key words are fun and comfort. Natural fabrics, dazzling colours, original details: cups with wings, lamps disguised as mirrors, rugs with words and messages on them. A dinner plate from the series "Aile-émoi" costs 430 francs; an ashtray, 750 francs.

Axis

Marché Saint-Germain, Saint-Sulpice entrance:
14, rue Lobineau, 75006.
☎ 01.43.29.66.23.
M° Mabillon.
Mon.-Sat. 10am-8pm.
13, Rue de Charonne, 75011. ☎ 01.48.06.79.10.
M° Bastille.
Tues.-Sat. 11am-7:30pm.

A store full of humour and poetry, where everyday objects are fun.

Crockery, vases, lights or rugs, given a new look by artists and illustrators. The Gideon by Benjamin Rabier was a source of

inspiration for a 1996 collection. Original plates, called "the flooded house", from 130 francs, lamps from 300 francs to 800 francs.

Miller et Bertaux

17, Rue Ferdinand-Duval, 75004.
☎ 01.42.78.28.39.
M° Hôtel-de-Ville.
Mon. 2-7pm; Tues.-Sat. 11am-1:30pm, 2-7pm.

Objects brought from all over the world and reworked by Miller et

Bertaux. Japanese-inspired flowing clothes and fragrances for the home. A unique, poetic store, where everything is chosen to appeal to the senses and emotions. Plenty of unusual things.

Xanadou

10, Rue Saint-Sulpice, 75006.
☎ 01.43.26.73.43.
M° Mabillon or Odéon.
Tues.-Sat. 11am-1pm, 2-7pm.

A store where you can find articles designed by architects from all over the world. A careful selection, intended to pass the test of time. Innovations, or rediscoveries like Macintosh cutlery (1904), the Malevitch teapot (1919) and Joseph Hoffmann glasses. Prices range from 120 francs for an Enzo Mari paper knife, to 5,000 francs for a crystal bowl by Borek Sipek.

AN OVERVIEW OF STYLE

Decorative enthusiasts may know the small book written by Philippe Jullian, *Les Styles*, published in 1960, and reprinted in 1992 with a supplement by Patrick Mauriès.
It's a light and witty history of the decorative arts.
The section on decoration since 1960 was written by Mauriès in his inimitably impertinent way, with beautiful illustrations by the fashion designer Christian Lacroix and plenty of references to amuse the cognoscenti. This work is a vivid portrayal of changing tastes and times, from the Knoll years to neo-Baroque, pop-art and punk.

FURNISHINGS, FABRICS AND BEAUTIFUL THINGS

Travellers often set out in search of new sensations; others merely dream of adventure, of exploring the unknown. Paris can offer you a world of hidden treasures: handwoven fabrics, furniture and ornaments made by local craftsmen, crockery, cashmere, embroidered cotton, wooden masks and wedding trousseaux. India, China, Japan, the Philippines, Thailand, Mexico, Africa; in Paris, you have the whole world at your feet.

The place to find designs by the Lebanese designer Lina Audi; stylised versions of nomadic and Mediterranean craftsmanship. A very pretty collection of drapes, household linen, tablecloths and bedspreads. Simple clothes, cotton bath towels. Soft, lovely Aleppo soap for 50 francs.

Caravane
6, Rue Pavée, 75004.
☎ 01.44.61. 04.20.
M° Saint-Paul.
Tues.-Sat. 11am-7pm.

Fabrics, rugs and objects from Asia or Africa (see p. 63).

Compagnie Française de l'Orient et de la Chine
260, Blvd Saint-Germain, 75007. ☎ 01.46.05.92.82.
M° Solférino.
Mon.-Sat. 10:30am-7pm.
163, 167, Blvd Saint-Germain, 75006. ☎ 01.45.48.00.18 and 01.45.48.10.31.
M° Saint-Germain-des-Prés.
Mon.-Sat. 10am-7pm.

You'll get a taste of China in these stores, from ceramics and the furniture of old Peking (at n° 260), to handicrafts (n° 167) and clothes (n°163). Cantonese red on plates, bowls, flowerpot holders, vases and jars. Traditional blue motifs hand-painted on porcelain (bowls for 17 francs). The blue cotton Mao jacket is still a fashion classic (295 francs); the smart city version in shantung costs 1,300 francs.

Liwan
8, Rue Saint-Sulpice, 75006.
☎ 01.43.26.07.40.
M° Saint-Sulpice.
Tues.-Fri. 10:30am-2pm, 3-7pm; Sat. 10:30am-7pm.

Le Jardin Moghol
53, Rue Vieille-du-Temple, 75004. ☎ 01.48.87.41.32.
M° Saint-Paul.
Tues.-Fri. 11am-7pm; Sat. 11am-7:30pm.

The silk route as if you were travelling it yourself, with these 15th- and 16th-century woven cotton and silk designs for bed and cushion covers, and tablecloths. Clothes, furniture, bits and pieces in a rainbow of colours. Beautiful drapes made from printed panels (525 francs; 140 by 280 cm), silk and wool stoles to wrap around you (from 490 francs).

L'ATELIER 74

Paris is a world capital worthy of its name, with a truly cosmopolitan feel. There are quite a number of stores that specialise in crafts, clothes and jewellery from all around the world. Parisians love the exotic touch. At Atelier 74, craftsmen from all over the world exhibit their work for a few weeks at a time: African jewellery, Amerindian fabrics, beads or leather, sculptures, precious objects or trinkets. The Atelier is a special place for the variety and wealth of inspiration reflected in the international artists and in their work.

L'Atelier 74, 74, Rue de la Verrerie, 75004.
M° Hôtel de Ville.

Galerie Bamyan
24, Rue Saint-Louis-en-l'Île, 75004.
☎ 01.46.33.69.66.
M° Pont Marie.
Tues.-Sat. 11:30-8pm; Sun. 2-8pm.

An anthropologist's treasures, the fruit of many travels. A place of exchange and discovery with handicrafts from central Asia and India. Traditional furniture adapted to modern tastes, wedding lists for the furniture, objects,

and jewellery of Indian brides. Coffee tables from 700 to 2,500 francs.

Le Monde Sauvage
101, Rue Saint-Denis, 75001.
☎ 01.40.26.28.81.
M° Étienne Marcel.
Mon. 1:30-7:30pm;
Tues.-Sat. 10:30am-7:30pm.

This store comes as a surprise in a street full of clothes boutiques and sex-shops. Antiques and copies of colonial furniture, along with objects from Asia or Central Europe. Wood, wrought iron, glass, wickerwork and fabrics. A small Indian wooden table costs 700 francs; 100 francs for a wrought-iron candleholder (with 5 candles).

La Ville de Mogador
16, Rue du Vieux-Colombier, 75006.
☎ 01.45.48.04.48.
M° Saint-Sulpice.
Mon.-Sat. 10am-2pm, 3-7pm.

This place has the atmosphere of an

oriental bazar, with rugs, pottery, Morrocan copper lanterns and hand-painted ceramic plates. Also, the familiar tea-glass that everyone loves costs 25 francs, an earthenware cooking pot costs from 250 to 600 francs.

Galerie Urubamba
4, Rue de la Bûcherie, 75005.
☎ 01.43.54.08.24.
M° Maubert-Mutualité.
Tues.-Sat. 2-7:30pm.

Named after the sacred valley of the Incas, this shop is where you can discover the crafts and traditions of tribes from the three Americas. Alpaca ponchos and embroidered blouses; Peruvian fabrics, ceramics and wickerwork. Beads, too, if you want to make your own jewellery. Books, cassettes and CDs. Authentic Indian mocassins for 300 francs.

THE LUXURY OF FINE LINEN

Lace-edged sheets for a romantic bed, tablecloths embroidered with floral patterns for a special dinner party; soft dressing gowns to keep warm in during the cold winter months, and towels in all sizes and colours. Spoil yourself in Paris, with its choice of the prettiest linen for your bedroom, bathroom or dining room. These shops are perfect places for wedding lists as well.

Atout Blanc

20, Rue de Rivoli, 75004.
☎ **01 48 04 98 50.**
M° Saint-Paul. Mon. 3-7pm;
Tues.-Fri. 11am-7pm; Sat.
10:30am-1:30pm, 2-7pm.

You'll find bath towels in more than 20 colours for 59 francs, superb dressing gowns (550 gr) for 299 francs, a wide range of quilt covers of all sizes, and tartan rugs for 99 francs. Nice products, nice prices.

Matin Bleu

92, Rue de Rennes, 75006.
☎ **01.42.22.94.40.**
M° Saint-Sulpice.
Mon.-Sat. 9am-7pm.

This store has four different lines for four lifestyles: "natural",

"modern", "nomadic" and "tender". There are Italian makes like Jalla and Bassetti, and a "Matin Bleu" range at

reasonable prices. For the bedroom, and the dining room too. Sheets for a double bed (94 by 118 inches) from 290 francs.

Blanc Cassé

101, Rue du Bac, 75007.
☎ **01.45.48.87.88.**
M° Sévres-Babylone.
Mon.-Sat. 10am-7pm.

Bath towels from 60 francs, dressing gowns for 220 francs, linen-and-cotton sheets for 460 francs. Seconds are unwrapped, but sold at unbeatable prices. A real bargain store.

Textures

55, Rue des Saints Pères, 75006.
☎ **01.45.48.90.88.**
M° Saint-Germain-des-Prés.
Mon. 14:30-6:30pm;
Tues.-Sat. 10am-6:30pm.

Worth a visit for the printed, dyed and embroidered Designers' Guild fabrics. Multicoloured bath sheets for 265 francs, bedding for babies, children and adults (sheets from 190 francs). Beautiful furnishing fabrics and even some sofas.

WHAT MAKES A GOOD TOWEL?

The ideal material is Egyptian cotton, or a cotton with long fibres. "Bouclé" was invented in the late 19th century: the loop is formed from the surplus left by a second weft thread. The more threads per square centimetre, the more loops there are, and the greater the quality of the towelling. In other words, heavy means luxurious (from 350 to 550 gr per square metre; after that, the fabric becomes too stiff). If towelling is shaved on one side, it changes in appearance and name: it becomes velvet.

La Paresse en Douce

97, Rue du Bac, 75007.
☎ 01.42.22.64.10.
M° Rue du Bac.
Tues.-Fri. 11am-7pm;
Sat. 2-7pm.

Cuddly flannelette for winter, silk and cotton for summer. Everything is soft, for lazing in luxury from bath to bed.

Slippers and pyjamas, soft dressing gowns and cushions, cool sheets and cashmere rugs. Tablecloths and tablemats. Embroidered towels from 120 francs, cushions for 240 francs.

Porthault

18, Ave. Montaigne, 75008.
☎ 01.47.20.75.25.
M° Alma-Marceau
or Franklin D. Roosevelt.
Mon. 9:30am-1pm,
2-6:30pm; Tues.-Fri.
9:30am-6:30pm; Sat.
9:30am-1pm, 2-6pm.

Luxury in the haute-couture neighbourhood: organdy, linen, silk and satin embroidered with leaves and flowers. The sheets, tablecloths, towels and robes are deliciously romantic, with lace openwork and panels. The "Studio" line is reasonably priced: 180 francs for a canvas tablemat, 300 francs for an embroidered towel.

Laurence Roque

69, Rue Saint-Martin, 75004.
☎ 01.42.72.22.12.
M° Châtelet. Tues.-Sat.
10:30am-6:30pm; Mon.
1:30-6:30pm, closed Sun.

This charming store specialises in bathroom and table linen, with various styles of embroidery and tapestry. Embroidery work from 50 to 800 francs. The nimble-fingered will find patterns, threads and fabrics for their favourite hobby here; others can console themselves by buying pre-embroidered articles, like bibs (about 60 francs each) or laundry bags. Once you've finished your masterpiece, you can also have it framed here. Mail-order service available.

Maison de Vacances

63, 64, Galerie de Montpensier, 75001.
☎ 01.47.03.99.74.
M° Palais-Royal-Musée du Louvre. Mon.-Fri. 1-7pm; Sat. noon-6pm (see p. 39).

SHOPPING FOR BARGAINS

If you don't insist on fashion that's "hot off the press" and are prepared to wear clothes from last season's collections, here are a few good places to know about.

FABRIC

Les Deux Portes

30, Blvd Henri-IV, 75011.
☎ 01.42.71.13.02. M° Bastille. Tues.-Sat. 10am-6:30pm.

A selection of fabrics at low prices, plus the popular "Deux Portes" line of fabrics. Twenty percent off quality collections (5 metres minimum). Year-round reductions, odd lots from 30 francs the metre. Ready-to-wear. Silk for furnishings, 250 francs the metre (140 cm wide).

Mendès

140, Rue Montmartre, 75002.
☎ 01.42.36.02.39.
M° Bourse.
Mon.-Fri. 10am-7pm; Sat. 10am-1pm, 2-6pm.

Fabrics made for Yves Saint Laurent and Christian Lacroix, straight from the factory. You'll have to wait 6 months after the fashion shows, but you'll pay up to 50 per cent less. Wool from 110 francs the metre, silks for 120 francs.

CLOTHES

Le Mouton à Cinq Pattes

8, 10, 18, 48,
Rue Saint-Placide, 75006.
☎ 01.45.55.13.09.
M° Sèvres-Babylone.
Mon.-Sat. 10:30am-7:30pm.
15, Rue Vieille-du-Temple, 75004. ☎ 01.42.71.86.30.
M° Hôtel-de-Ville.
Lun. 2-7:30pm; Tues.-Fri. 10:30am-7:30pm (closed 2-3pm); Sat. 11am-8pm.

A well-known Parisian address, a classic of its kind, with top quality ready-to-wear from manufacturers all over Europe. The collections arrive here two or three weeks after they've been delivered to the fashion boutiques. Fashionable, but not over the top. Blazers from 299 to 800 francs. Women's and children's wear, and men's wear at the annex (n° 48).

L'Annexe des Créateurs

19, Rue Godot de Mauroy, 75009.
☎ 01.42.65.46.40.
M° Madeleine.
Mon.-Sat. 10:30am-7pm.

All year round, 40 to 70 per cent off designer and couturier collections. Last season's styles, from designer business suits to cocktail dresses. Wonderful accessories, plus wedding dresses and a men's wear department. From 390 francs for a skirt and 990 francs for a suit.

Chercheminippes

109, 110, 111, Rue du Cherche-Midi, 75006.
☎ 01.42.22.45.23.
M° Duroc.
Mon.-Sat. 10:30am-6pm (consignment), 7pm (sales).

FEET STREET

The Rue Meslay (métro Strasbourg-Saint-Denis) has more shoe shops than anywhere else in Paris, with retailers, manufacturers and wholesalers located side by side. The following is one of many interesting places to shop:
Mart-ine, 63, Rue Meslay, 75003, 01.42.71.35.09.
Mon-Sat 9am-7pm.
The most fashionable shoes, up-to-the-minute styles for 20 to 30 per cent less than elsewhere. *Doc Martens, Timberland, Converse* and *Caterpillars*. Low Doc Martens from 400 francs, hightops from 480 francs.

A practical consignment store. The clothes you'll find here are no more than a year old. Women's wear at n° 109 (Kenzo, Klein etc). New clothes and haute-couture at n° 111 (Chanel, Hermès etc). At n° 110, men's and children's wear. Irié jackets for 580 francs, Aridza Bross T-shirts for 60 francs. Everything is half-price.

Tati

2-42, Blvd Rochechouart, 75018. ☎ 01.42.55.13.09.
M° Barbès-Rochechouart.
Mon. 10am7pm;
Tues.-Fri. 9:30am-7pm;
Sat. 9:15am-7pm.

Everybody knows about the Tati stores. People even come from

Eastern European countries to do their shopping here. Everyone sneaks a peek to see the new goods, even if they don't admit it. The Tati line "La Rue est

à Nous" is young and trendy, with jumpers from 79 francs; there's also a children's range called "L'Avenir est à Nous", with waffle-cloth and cotton piqué T-shirts. Go for the atmosphere on Saturday mornings; it's like crossing the Mediterranean without leaving Paris.

Guerrisold

29-31, Ave. de Clichy, 75017.
☎ 01.53.42.31.32.
M° Place de Clichy.
Mon.-Sat. 10am-7:30pm.
17 bis, Blvd Rochechouart, 75018.
☎ 01.45.26.38.92.
M° Barbès.
Mon.-Sat. 9:30am-7pm.

You'll find a huge selection of old clothes and new at unbeatably low prices. Don't hesitate to go in and browse around; no two items are the same, whatever the size. The "Delta" line is young and trendy. Shirts from 19 francs to 69 francs; silk shirts start at 50 francs; and suits from 50 to 120 francs.

COMPUTERS

Surcouf

139, Ave. Daumesnil, 75012.
☎ 01.53.33.20.00.
M° Gare de Lyon.
Tues.-Sat. 9:30am-7pm.

France's largest computer store, with 300 demonstrators,

RUE D'ALÉSIA: BARGAINS FOR READY-TO-WEAR

A few stores along a section of the Rue d'Alésia (métro Alésia) have specialised in ready-to-wear designer seconds for the last 15 years.

■ **Cacharel Stock**, at n°114 ☎ 01.45.42.53.04, has a selection of men's, women's and children's wear (a wide range of shirts from 220 francs).

■ **Dorotennis**, at n° 74, for chic sportswear, coordinates and swimwear (from 50 to 169 francs).

■ **Régina Rubens**, 88, rue d'Alésia, 75014, ☎ 01.40.44.90.05.

■ **Daniel Hechter** (Stock 2), at n° 92, ☎ 01.45.41.65.57, for styles for last season's collections, clothes and accessories for men, women and children.

■ The **Évolutif** shop (at n° 139, ☎ 01.45.45.44.83) has a wide range of men's clothes (Cerruti suits from 1,800 francs, Kenzo pullovers 700 francs).

250 stands and an exhibition area of 10,000 m2. They've got every imaginable item for your computing needs (microcomputer, printers, other peripherals, discs, books). There's a consignment store, as well as a "computer flea market" where you can sometimes find real bargains.

A GOURMET'S PARADISE

You'll find the finest produce from all over the world in Paris, with a marvellous selection of the best of everything from spices to condiments, chocolates and teas. Not to mention the most unusual fruits, the most exotic flavours and the best home-grown specialities. You can find everything you want all year round, and at Christmas time you'll be spoilt for choice.

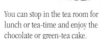

You can stop in the tea room for lunch or tea-time and enjoy the chocolate or green-tea cake.

Mariage Frères

30, Rue du Bourg-Tibourg, 75004.
☎ **01.42.72.28.11.**
M° Hôtel-de-Ville.
Daily 10:30am-7:30pm;
tea room, noon-7pm.

This is a wonderful store with hundreds of tins of tea piled up on dark wooden shelves. The sales staff are experts and will always take the time to guide you in your choice.
A Mariage line of teapots and teacups, adapted from traditional Chinese and Japanese shapes.

La Boutique jaune

58, Rue Henri Barbusse, 75005.
☎ **01 40.46.05.90.**
M° Port-Royal.
Mon.Fri. 10am-8pm;
Sat. 10:30am-2pm.

Parisians generally have their roots in provincial France, and they love the authentic savours of their rural origins. Every neighbourhood has its own grocer with regional products, and connoisseurs recommend good addresses to each other. La Boutique Jaune (near the RER station at Port-Royal) is one of the most recent, with excellent products from Brittany and southwest France: it offers pâtés and sausages, salmon and tinned foods. The service is friendly; and you can order and eat on the premises all day long.

Debauve et Gallais

30, Rue des Saints-Pères, 75006.
☎ **01.45.48.54.67.**
M° Saint-Germain-des-Prés.
33, Rue Vivienne, 75002.
☎ **01.40.39.05.50.**
M° Bourse.
Mon.-Sat. 9:30am-6:30pm.

Marvellous wooden counters and chocolates lined up in battle order. The store once supplied goods to Louis XVIII and Charles X. Debauve invented sugar-free chocolate, vanilla chocolate, orange blossom chocolate— items still sold today, for 95 francs the box. The latest product, called "l'Incroyable" (the incredible), is a nougatine filled with ganache. A 300-gr box costs 148 francs.

L'Herboristerie du Palais-Royal

11, Rue des Petits-Champs, 75001.
☎ **01.42.97.54.68.**
M° Palais-Royal-Musée du Louvre.
Mon.-Fri. 9am-7pm.

Natural wood and wickerwork create a lovely backdrop for the hundreds of medicinal and aromatic plants in the shops. Cosmetics made from plant extracts, essential oils for hair, face and body. Rose and jasmine fragrances for your bath or your home. A packet of mallow flowers costs 30 francs, and wheatgerm oil is priced at 78 francs per 100 ml.

Faguais

30, Rue de La Trémoille, 75008.
☎ **01.47.20.80.91.**
M° George-V.
Mon.Sat. 9:15am-7pm.

This old-style store, where the cash register is still behind a glass partition, has been importing the best Arabica coffee since 1912. Ethiopian mocha, Salvadorian pacarama, Jamaican blue mountain. The coffee is roasted as needed, and costs from 30.50 francs for 250 gr. The store also sells

traditional fine groceries, including superb teas and delicious honeys.

Verlet

256, Rue Saint-Honoré, 75001.
☎ **01.42.60.67.39.**
M° Palais-Royal-Musée du Louvre.
Tues.-Sat. 9am-7pm (winter); Mon.-Fri. 9am-7pm (May-Oct.).

Where coffee is an art, like poetry or music. They create their own blends that change with the seasons: milder in summer, stronger in autumn. You can taste freshly roasted coffee on the spot: Arabica from Jamaica, Hawaï and Columbia, and 20 or so Verlet varieties. Teas, dried and candied fruits and ice-creams. From 25 to 48 francs for 100 gr.

Olsen Bornholm

8, Rue du Commandant Rivière, 75008.
☎ **01.45.61.22.64.**
M° St-Philippe-du-Roule.
Mon.-Fri. 9am-8pm; Sat. 10am-7pm.

Products imported from the Baltic. Eels for 260 francs a kilo, smoked wild salmon for 280 francs a kilo: Parisian Scandinavians all come here! Exceptional marzipan for 180 francs a kilo. There are a few tables if you can't wait to get it home.

THE BEST . . .

■ FAUCHON
26, Pl. de la Madeleine, 75008,
☎ 01.47.42.60.11.
M° Madeleine. Mon.-Sat. 9:40am-7pm; caterer 9:30pm. Where else can you find honey (100 francs a pot) made by bees from the Garnier Opera that have gathered pollen from the flowers in the Tuileries gardens? Preserves, liqueurs, jams, sauces, all kinds of delicious things. Mail-order possible from abroad.

■ HÉDIARD,
21, Pl. de la Madeleine, 75008,
☎ 01.43.12.88.88.
M° Madeleine. Mon.-Sat. 9:30am-9pm. The other famous delicatessen on the Place de la Madeleine; a great classic (see p. 36).

■ IZRAEL, 30, Rue François Miron, 75004,
☎ 01.42.72.66.23. M° Saint-Paul. Tues.-Fri. 9:30am-1pm, 2:30-7pm; Sat. 9:30am-1pm. Rare, aromatic spices, the magic of the Orient in the heart of the Marais (see p. 58).

ALL KINDS OF MARKETS

Parisian markets date back to the Middle Ages. Many of them still supply the capital with food for the body and the spirit! This selection includes the particularly picturesque and unusual markets.

FOOD

Tang Frères

48, Ave d'Ivry, 75013. M° Porte d'Ivry. Daily 9am-7:30pm; closed Mon.

An incredible Asian supermarket, usually very crowded. Chinese cabbage, kumquats, Basmati rice, sticky rice, 100-year-old eggs, dim sum (20 francs the dozen), meat, fish, bonsais, crockery, Chinese beer, ready-made dishes (10 francs for 100 gr). Colour, atmosphere, and unbeatable prices. For the price of a métro ticket, spend a Sunday afternoon in the Far East when the rest of Paris is closed.

Belleville market

On the central section dividing the Blvd de Belleville, 75020. M° Belleville. Tues., Fri. 7am-1:30pm.

People come here from all over Paris to find plantains, yams and chayotes. Plenty of exotic fruits; indeed, many West Indian, African, and Asian restaurants stock up here. A wide selection of fresh herbs and spices. Wend your way among the women in boubous, enjoy the exotic atmosphere and tempting aromas.

Organic market

Blvd Raspail, between Rue du Cherche-Midi and Rue de Rennes, 75006. M° Sèvres-Babylone or Rennes. Sun. morning.

All the Left-Bank ecologists and Parisian health-food freaks frequent this pretty market with its organically grown produce. The prices are on the high side, but you will find all kinds of

vegetables, such as squash, pumpkin and Chinese cabbage. Charcuterie stalls and regional products.

Mouffetard market

Rue Mouffetard, as far as the Place de la Contrescarpe, 75005. M°Censier-Daubenton. Tues.-Sat. 9am-1pm, 4-9:30pm; Sun. morning.

Parisians call this market "La Mouff". It's famous for its fruit, vegetables and charcuterie. With its colourful stalls, old church and accordionist,

it looks like a film set: Paris as you've always imagined it (with, unfortunately, rather a lot of tourists). A nice place for a Sunday-morning outing.

Aligre market

Rue d'Aligre, 75012.
M° Ledru-Rollin.
Daily 8am-1pm, 3-30-
7:30pm; Sun. 8am-1pm;
closed Mon.

Although it's not far from the trendy Bastille district, the Place d'Aligre is still an authentic Parisian market, mostly run by North African stall-holders. The Beauveau market is a beautiful 19th-century covered market, worth a visit for its paving stones and fountain. An excellent charcuterie and exceptional cheese merchant. Several secondhand clothes stalls too.

FABRIC

Marché Saint-Pierre

2, Rue Charles-Nodier,
75018.
☎ 01.46.06.92.25.
M° Anvers.
Tues.-Sat. 9:15am-8:30pm;
Mon. 1-6:30pm.

This big fabric store is a paradise for dressmakers and do-it-yourself enthusiasts. The silks department

THE BIRD AND FLOWER MARKET

Place Louis-Lépine,
75001.
M° Cité.
Lun.-sam. de 8h à 19h30.

A stone's throw from the Palais de Justice, the Ile de la Cité is covered in flowers: primroses, geraniums, rhododendrons and hydrangeas, plus a good selection of bonsais. The bird market takes over, Sundays from 8am to 7.30pm: listen to the trill of canaries, mina birds, budgerigars and rare birds. If you have children, continue your walk across the Seine; on the other side, Quai de la Mégisserie, there are pet shops and shops where you can see fish from all over the world (open Sundays).

on the second floor is the best in Paris. Furnishing fabrics on the third floor, household linen on the fourth. Prices start at 20 francs for 2 metres of woollen fabric.

The **Reine** store just across the street specialises in furnishing fabrics.
The surrounding streets are lined with fabric retail outlets, and you'll find a larger selection of fabrics in this area than anywhere else in the entire country.

BOOKS AND STAMPS

Book market

Rue Brancion, 75015.
M° Porte de Vanves.
Sat. and Sun. 9:30am-6pm.

The Georges Brassens park is a meeting place every weekend for impoverished intellectuals and book-lovers. Secondhand books for 10 francs, comic strips, and vintage editions of *Tintin* or rare books are all to be found in this covered market, which is a treasure hunter's delight.

Stamp market

On the corner of Ave.
Marigny and Ave. Gabriel,
75008. M° Franklin D.
Roosevelt. Thurs. Sat. Sun.
and holidays.

This open-air Parisian institution is the favourite meeting place for philatelists and telephone-card collectors. You may well find the missing piece to add to your collection, but you have to be prepared to pay for it. There is a large selection of old postcards as well, classified according to theme or region, to get an idea of what Paris looked like at the turn of the century.

FLEA MARKETS AND ANTIQUES

With more than 4,000 antique or secondhand dealers and the largest auction room in the country, Paris and the surrounding area is the heart of France's national art market. You can buy or sell everything from teddy bears to sedan chairs. Every weekend, put your credit cards away and get ready to haggle!

Hôtel Drouot

9, Rue Drouot, 75009.
☎ 01.48.00.20.20.
M° Richelieu-Drouot.
Objects are displayed the day before the sale 11am-6pm and the morning of the sale 11am-noon; sales 2-6pm.

You can save a lot of money by buying at an auction rather than from an antique-dealer; auction sales are often where the dealers find their goods anyway. Beware though, you must add about 11 per cent to the price of the final bid. All auction sales are advertised in *La Gazette de l'hôtel Drouot* (13.50 francs from news-stands). The lots for sale are put on display for viewing prior to the sale; take your time and look at each piece carefully; you're free to pick up objects you're interested in. If you're not present on the day of the auction, you can leave a buying order with the auctioneer. The item will be yours if the price you have determined is not overbid. There are no auctions in Paris at weekends, but there may be at Versailles or Saint-Germain. In any case, you'll find them all in *La Gazette*.

Saint-Ouen flea market

M° Porte de Clignancourt.
Sat., Sun., Mon. 8am-6pm.

The Saint-Ouen flea market consists of several different and quite separate markets, and is the largest area in the world devoted to the sale of antiques. People come from all over to hunt down a specific object or just to look around. It's a favourite Sunday outing for Parisians all year round, and it's especially popular with tourists during the summer months. Don't expect to find great bargains, but don't expect to be swindled either. You'll find all sorts of things, more or less at the going price in Paris. The salespeople know their stuff, and if you find the prices high, it's no doubt because there are customers willing to pay those prices. However, you can always negotiate the price of the piece of furniture or object that interests you; a discount of 10 per cent on the asking price is quite common, and if you insist you can even bring the price down 25 or

30 per cent. All the stallholders work with carriers who can arrange delivery throughout the world. Check the prices, though, as delivery will push the price up.

Paul Bert market
Rue Paul Bert.

This just may be the last flea market where you can still find authentic secondhand stalls. Ironware, garden furniture, objects from the 1950s and 1960s, glassware and earthenware.

Biron market
Rue des Rosiers.

This market has two distinct sides: the covered alley specialises in good quality rustic and bourgeois regional furniture (a lot of fruit-tree wood), while the open-air alley is much more flashy, with lots of crystal lights and period furniture with gilded bronzes. A few stalls deal in Art Nouveau and Art Deco objects, and you can find fans and glassware as well.

There is a carrier at the market entrance, which is practical if you buy something cumbersome.

Rosiers market
Rue Paul-Bert.

Molten glass and ceramic objects from the turn of the century. Plenty of Lalique, Gallé and Decorchemont; everything is beautiful, everything is expensive.

Serpette market
Rue des Rosiers.

A recent market, with plenty of Art Deco and Art Nouveau objects, paintings and furniture, although not always restored in the best of taste. Plus, prices are rather high.

Jules Vallès market
Rue Jules-Vallès.

Old postcards, old toys, garden furniture and great collections of attic bric-a-brac. Nearby, there are several stores which sell odd bits and pieces of metal: sheets of cast iron, balcony railings, spiral staircases and old bathtubs.

Vernaison market
Ave. Michelet.

A big hotchpotch of a market with a maze of irregular alleyways. Good for rugs, regional earthenware, bibelots and ornaments. Standard regional furniture. An amusing stall that sells old spectacles.

Malassis market
Rue des Rosiers.

The stores in this new, light and airy Saint-Ouen market reflect whatever is back in vogue: Art Deco, 1950s, Napoleon III. There are not many large items of furniture, mostly small china or

barbotine ornaments, paintings and sculptures. Prices are on the high side.

Dauphine market
Rue des Rosiers.

On two storeys: engravings, paintings, ornaments, beautiful furniture from the 18th century to the 1950s, earthenware and porcelain, old books and papers.

Montreuil flea market
**Ave. du Professeur-André-Lemierre, 75020.
M° Porte de Montreuil.
Sat., Sun., Mon. 8am-6pm.**

Some standard secondhand objects, generally of no great interest, and some great 1960s and 1970s clothes: have fun dressing up for next to nothing.

Vanves flea market
**Ave. Georges-Lafenestre, 75014.
M° Porte de Vanves.
Sat. and Sun. 7am-7:30pm.**

Good general stalls (bibelots, curios, books, earthenware), paintings and household furniture from the late 1800s to the present day. This market is considerably cheaper than Saint-Ouen (antique dealers themselves stock up here). The perfect place for unearthing an unusual treasure. Our favourite market.

Night-life

Paris is no more dangerous at night than anywhere else. Certain areas are best avoided after 1am. These include Stalingrad, Barbès and Les Halles (which can be a bit suspect late at night), but on the whole you'll have nothing to fear. The last métro isn't always the best place to make friends, but it's pretty safe. Here are a few ideas and addresses to make your life easier.

TRAVELLING AROUND AT NIGHT

Métro: All the métro lines operate from 5.30am to about 1am, when the last train leaves the station.

Bus: The following buses run till half past midnight: 21, 26, 27, 31, 38, 52, 62, 63, 72, 74, 80, 82, 85, 91, 92, 95, 96, PC. Timetables are displayed in the bus shelters; buses usually come every 15 or 30 minutes. Other bus services stop at about 8.30 to 9pm.

The RATP (Parisian transport authority) has started up a *Noctambus* service, which leaves from Place Victoria (Châtelet) every hour between 1.30 and 5.30am (from the terminus, between 1 and 5am). It costs three tickets, or 7.50 francs. Only the west of Paris is not covered by these night routes.

Taxi: About 2,000 of the 15,500 or so taxi drivers work at night. It's best to phone for a taxi, but you can often get one from a taxi rank or stop one in the street. The pick-up fee (at a rank) is 13 francs. From 7pm until 7am, and on Sundays and bank holidays, tariff B is in operation (5.45 francs the kilometre).

If you go out to the suburbs (the Hauts-de-Seine, Val-de-Marne and Seine-Saint-Denis), tariff B is used from 7am to 7pm, and C (7 francs the kilometre) from 7pm to 7am, as well as Sundays and bank holidays.

If you ask a taxi driver to wait for you, the charge is 130 francs per hour. If you want to do a tour of Paris by night to see the lights, it will cost you about 75 francs for 30 minutes.

Limousine: So you want to play the VIP (even if it means emptying your piggy-bank)? Contact International Limousines, 182, Blvd Péreire, 75017, ☎ 01.53.81.14.00. From 8pm to midnight, you'll have a chauffeur and a Mercedes 300 SEL (four-door) or a Silverstar six-door for 1,910 francs (inclusive of tax). On Sundays, you'll have to pay a weekend supplement of 110 francs: peanuts!

WHAT'S ON AND HOW TO FIND OUT ABOUT IT?

Most daily papers, such as *le Figaro, le Monde* and *Libération*, have

fairly complete entertainment pages. The Bible for entertainment info is still *Pariscope* (3 francs) or *l'Officiel des Spectacles* (2 francs), both of which come out Wednesdays. This is also the day new movies come out and the programmes change.

WHAT TIME DO PEOPLE GO OUT?

To dinner: Starting at 8pm. Some restaurants have two sittings and serve meals until late at night.

To cafés: From 6 or 8pm. To the opera, often 7.30pm. To the theatre, at 8.30 or 9pm. Concerts often start at 8.30pm; night clubs, not before 11 or 11.30pm.

WHAT TO WEAR?

If you're going to eat in a top-notch restaurant, you should wear a jacket and tie, or a suit. People rarely dress up for the opera or theatre nowadays, except on opening nights. If you go clubbing, wear whatever's in fashion (with or without tie, it varies).

In trendy bars, pubs or cafés, dress however you like. Sneakers, however, are not always appreciated.

FOR NIGHT OWLS

If you have an irresistible urge to see a movie at midnight, check out the programs of the UGC cinemas on the Champs-Élysées, or the Gaumont cinemas in Montparnasse and at the Étoile, and at the Publicis Élysées.

Feeling peckish? The Ancienne Comédie bakery (10, Rue de l'Ancienne-Comédie, 75006, ☎ 01.43.26.89.72) is open 24 hours a day.

Desperate to hear some jazz? Champs Disques (84, Ave des Champs-Élysées, 75008) is open Monday to Saturday, 9am to midnight; Sundays, noon to 8pm. The Virgin Megastore (at n° 52, Ave des Champs-Élysées ☎ 01.49.53.50.00) is open 10am to midnight, Sundays from noon to midnight.

KEEPING UP WITH THE NEWS

The following news-stands are open non-stop: 33 and 60, Champs-Élysées; Place de l'Etoile; and16, Blvd de la Madeleine.

The Prisunic at 109, Rue la Boétie, ☎ 01.42.25.27.46, is open till midnight; the **Drugstores Publicis** at 133, Ave des Champs-Élysées (☎ 01.44.43.79.00), and 1, Ave Matignon (☎ 01.43.59.38.70) are open daily from 8.30am to 2am.

LAST-MINUTE TICKETS

You can get half-price theatre tickets (depending on the number of seats available) for same-day shows from the following places: the **kiosque de la Madeleine** (daily, noon-8pm; Sun. to 4pm); the **kiosque du Chatelet** (12.30-4pm, except Sun. and bank holidays); the **kiosque de Montparnasse** (12.30-8pm; Sun. to 4pm). For other shows (concerts, exhibitions, sporting events and so on) you can try your luck at the **FNAC** agencies (Mon.-Sat. 10am-7.30pm) and at **Virgin** (Mon.-Sat. 10am-midnight; Sun., noon-midnight). **Ticket +** proposes an easy solution for all kinds of shows (theatre, concerts, cabarets, sporting events, exhibitions and theme parks): You choose your show and pay by check or credit card. Your tickets will then be sent by mail, or you can pick them up at a Billetel outlet. For information and reservations, 7 days a week: ☎ 3615 BILLETEL.

If you need some bedtime reading, don't forget the bookstore at the **Virgin Megastore;** or **Mots à la Bouche,** 6, Rue Sainte-Croix-de-la-Bretonnerie, ☎ 01.42.78.88.30. (open till 11pm, Mon. to Sat.); **l'Écume des Pages,** 174, Blvd Saint-Germain, 75006, 01.45.48.54.48, open till midnight (closed Sun.); **La Hune,** 170, Blvd Saint-Germain, 75006, ☎ 01.45.48.35.85., open till midnight (closed Sun.); the **Marché Saint-André,** 40, Rue Saint-André-des-Arts, 75006, ☎ 01.43.26.16.03, also open till midnight.

NIGHT-LIFE

Where should you go when you have only 48 hours in the City of Light? A concert or an opera? A friendly café or a cool-and-trendy one? Dance music or jazz? An Irish pub or a night-club? Choose what suits your mood of the moment. Some of the following addresses are somewhat away from the city-centre; the current in-places stretch from the Bastille to the heights of Belleville or Ménilmontant. World culture is the vogue, world music is the sound: go out and explore!

The lights of the city

There are two ways of seeing the lights of Paris: on land or from the water. You can take the riverside expressway from the Maison de la Radio to Bercy. You'll pass Trocadéro, opposite the Eiffel Tower, to reach Place de la Concorde; then drive alongside the Tuileries Gardens. The Orsay Museum is on the opposite bank. Don't take the underground route or you'll miss the newly renovated dome of the Institut de France on the left bank. A little farther on, you'll see the beautiful, classical colonnade of the Louvre Museum. Keep an eye open for La Samaritaine department store, a monument to Art Deco. The Pont neuf on your right is also illuminated. After that, you'll see the long façade of the Conciergerie on the Île de la Cité. Then you arrive at the Place du Châtelet, where the Palmier fountain plays between the two theatres. On the Île de la Cite is the dome of the Tribunal de Commerce. The imposing Notre-Dame Cathedral then looms up. The brightly lit Place de l'Hôtel de Ville awaits you next, after

which you arrive in the Marais, with its marvellous old buildings and beautiful façades. Look across to the opposite bank; you're approaching the Île Saint-Louis, with its wonderful 17th-century mansions. Then go under the Austerlitz bridge and along the riverside through the Bercy district. To view Paris from th'e Seine, you can take a boat trip or a dinner-cruise, depending on your taste and your purse.

Bateaux Parisiens

☎ 01.44.11.33.55, Port de la Bourdonnais (in front of the Eiffel Tower). Free parking for three hours, access via the Quai Branly opposite the Avenue de la Bourdonnais. An hour-long trip, departures every 30 minutes, 10am to 10:30pm (except at 7:30pm); 45 francs per person, 20 francs for the under-twelves. Dinner cruise (560 francs! 8:30 to 11pm with classical music (orchestra and singer). The boat goes from Bercy to the Statue of Liberty. Dress: smart.

Parisian yachts: the *Don Juan*

A 1930s boat with mahogany and teak fittings, and a black marble fireplace in the large lounge. There is an officers' wardroom and comfortable armchairs.

A food-lover's cruise, with a menu dreamed up by Gérard Besson. Lobster salads, aiguillette of beef, foie gras and more. Price: 790 francs per person with a half-bottle of wine; the boat leaves at 9pm and returns around 11pm.

Concerts

Salle Pleyel
252, Rue du Faubourg Saint-Honoré, 75008.
☎ 01.45.61.53.00.
M° Ternes.

The philarmonic orchestra of Radio France plays on Fridays at 8pm. Pasdeloup concerts on Saturdays at 5:30pm. Lamou-

reux concerts on Sundays at 5:45pm. Performances from 30 September through 20 June. Telephone reservations Monday to Friday 9am to 6pm, two weeks in advance; tickets direct from the box office (11am to 6pm); the day of the concert just before it begins; or by mail with a stamped, self-addressed envelope. Ticket prices range from 65 to 190 francs.

Cité de la Musique
221, Ave. Jean-Jaurès, 75019. M° Pantin.
Programme:
☎ 01.44.84.44.84.
Architecture by Christian de Portzamparc, with a concert hall, museum amphitheatre and the "street of music" (free concerts). Reservations by mail at least 3 weeks in advance; by phone or at the box office daily from noon to 6pm, Sunday 10am to 6pm.

You can sometimes get tickets at the box office 30 minute before a concert. The repertory includes classical and baroque music, jazz, rock, traditional French songs and contemporary creations.

 Le chant

Opéra Garnier
Pl. de l'Opéra, 75009.
M° Opéra.

Opéra Bastille
120, Rue de Lyon, 75012.
M° Bastille.
Location
☎ 08.36.69.78.68.

Purchase tickets (at the theatre or via an agency) well in advance. The reopening of the Opéra Garnier means a more extensive programme, which will appeal to a wider audience. Tickets from 60 to 590 francs.

Péniche Opéra

Opposite 200,
Quai de Jemmapes, 75010.
M° Jaurès. ☎
01.42.45.18.20
Mon. to Fri. 11am-8pm;
Sat. 2-8pm; Sun. 2-5pm. Closed
15 July-15
Aug.

A renovated barge near the Hôtel du Nord. Performances at 9pm, Sundays at 5pm. The productions and shows are taken from classical and contemporary repertoires. Tickets from 60 to 250 francs.

Jazz

La Villa

29, Rue Jacob, 75006.
☎ 01.43.26.60.00.
M° Saint-Germain-des-Prés.
Daily 10:30pm.
Closed Sun. and August.

In the basement of a 4-star hotel with a modern decor by Marie-Christine Dorner. There is a new programme every week, with quartets and quintets, American and European artists, a wide range of genres and some well-known names, including Ceccarelli, Roney, Van Freeman, Kurt Elling. New talents are welcome as well. Admission: 120 france including one drink, 150 francs on Friday and Saturday.

Le Duc des Lombards

42, Rue des Lombards, 75001.
☎ 01.42.33.22.88.
M° Châtelet.

Improvisations, Latin American and French jazz in a wood and red-velvet decor. Concerts at 10pm, 9pm on Sundays. Admission is 70 francs on weekdays, 80 francs on Fridays and Saturdays.

Le Baiser Salé

58, Rue des Lombards, 75001.
☎ 01.42.33.37.71.
7pm-6am; jazz at 10:30pm, Sun. at 9pm.

A wide range of jazz from Africa, South America, Usa and Europe. Thurs., Fri. and Sat.: contemporary French songs at 8pm. Admission from 30 to 70 francs.

Le Sunset

60, Rue des Lombards
☎ 01.40.26.46.60.
9:30pm to dawn,
concert at 10:30pm.

Opened in 1976, it's now the oldest club in the street. Acoustic jazz, predominantly bop, with Christian Vander, the Belmondo Brothers, Laurent de Wilde. Sun.: local jazz; Mon.: Latin jazz; Tues.: new-generation jazz; Wed. to Sat.: international groups. Admission from 50 to 80 francs.

Le New Morning

7/9, Rue des Petites-Écuries, 75010. ☎ 01.45.23.51.41.
M° Château d'Eau.
Doors open at 8pm, concerts at 9pm; reservations: 5-7pm and after 8pm.

An institution, with all the big names in jazz from Art Blakey to Dizzy Gillespie. The decor looks something like a converted garage. Salsa, blues, Afro, rock and a variety of live music. Admission about 110 francs.

Pubs

Kitty O'Shea

10, Rue des Capucines, 75002.
☎ 01.40.15.00.30.
M° Opéra.
Daily noon-1:30am.

Welcome to Ireland in Paris, where you can watch live satellite TV coverage of Irish sporting matches on Sundays at 3pm. People of all ages crowd in at weekends. Live music on Sunday evenings at 8pm; 35 francs for a whisky

The Frog & Rosbif

116, Rue Saint-Denis, 75002.
☎ 01.42.36.34.73.
M° Étienne-Marcel.
Daily noon-2am.

Very British indeed. English beer is brewed on the premises. A regular crowd, both French and Anglophone. Acide jazz and funk in a relaxed atmosphere. A half-pint costs 22 francs, a pint 35 francs, and a jug 100 francs. Brunch on Sundays, noon to 4pm.

Trendy bars in chic quartiers

In the last few months, the epicentre of trendy Parisian nightlife has migrated towards the 11th *arrondissement*, between République and Père-Lachaise. Wander over there to discover the authentically trendy Paris.

Café-Charbons

109, Rue Oberkampf,
75011. ☎ 01.43.57.55.13.
M° Parmentier.
Daily 9am-2am. Brunch Sat. and Sun. noon-5pm.

Le Cithéa

114, Rue Oberkampf.
75011. ☎ 01.40.21.70.95.

La Mercerie

98, Rue Oberkampf
☎ 01.43.38.81.30.

Le Troisième Bureau

74, Rue de la Folie-Méricourt. 75011. ☎ 01.43.55.87.65.

Le Satellit'café

44, Rue de la Folie-Méricourt, 75011.
☎ 01.47.00.48.87.

La Perla

26, Rue François-Miron, 75004.
☎ 01.42.77.59.40.
M° Saint-Paul.
Daily noon-2am.

Le Camelot

50, Rue Amelot, 75011.
☎ 01.43.55.54.04.

Le Clown Bar

114, Rue Amelot, 75011.
☎ 01.43.55.87.35.

Les Couleurs

117, Rue Saint-Maur 75011.
☎ 01.43.57.95.61.
M° Parmentier or Saint-Maur.
Daily 2pm-2am.

At the intersection of Rue Oberkampf and Rue Saint-Maur, between the métro stations Parmentier and Ménilmontant, is the current heart of Paris nightlife. In the last few months, a flurry of bars have opened; some are already fashionable, others less so, but these are perhaps more authentic. Les Couleurs is one of our favourites. Go for the Tango morning sessions (Saturdays) or the concerts of Swing, jazz and African music (Fridays, Saturdays and Sundays). The ambience is great: artists, young actors and students.

Le Cannibale Café

93, Rue Jean-Pierre-Timbaud at the corner of the Rue du Moulin-Joli, 75011.
☎ 01.49.29.95.59.
M° Couronne.
Daily 7am-2am.

An eclectic café which attracts a mix of cultures and ages. Brasserie-style lunch where artists and the cinema crowd mingle with the locals under a decor of salvaged chandeliers and mirrors. Background music and cocktails from 37 francs.

La Flèche d'or

102 bis, Rue de Bagnolet 75020. ☎ 01.43.72.04.23.
M° Gambetta or Porte de Bagnolet.
Open daily except Mon. 10am-2am.

FLÈCHE D'OR CAFÉ

The small train no longer runs along the railway line that ran around Paris and under the old Bagnolet Station. The track, overgrown with weeds and flowers, is now a hunting-ground for the local cats. The station itself, suspended above rails, has been converted into a lively bistro. It's frequented by local artists and trendies, the young and not-so-young. There's live music Saturday evenings, and the beer is a lot cheaper than in Montparnasse or at the Bastille—what's more, there's not a tourist in sight. Brunch on Sundays.

Le China Club

50, Rue de Charenton, 75012.
☎ **01.43.43.82.02.**
M° Ledru-Rollin.
Open daily 7pm-2am; Fir and Sat to 3:30am.

Stepping across the threshold is like stepping into a luxurious

club in colonial Hong Kong or Saigon. The first part of the room is the restaurant, but the bar at the back is particularly spectacular, with comfortable sofas, high windows, and an incredibly long counter. The perfect place for a Long Island Iced Tea with your lady or gentleman-friend. On the first floor, take a look at the bathroom, and sit in the "smoking room" (more intimate and cosy than the

ground floor), to listen to an operatic aria. An exotic and sophisticated change of scene. It makes you feel as if you're on a film set.

Lou Pascalou

14,Rue des Panoyaux, 75020. ☎ **01.46.36.78.10. M° Ménilmontant. Open daily 9:30am-2am.**

This old bistro has recently been rejuvenated, but its décor—like something straight out of a post-war realist movie—remains unchanged. The local drunkards from this likeable, working-class district have been replaced by unpretentious young artists and budding actors. There is a good, relaxed atmosphere, and you can even have a game of French billiards.

Le Soleil

136, Boulevard de Ménilmontant 75020.
☎ **01.46.36.47.44.**
M° Ménilmontant.
Daily 8am-2am.

News of the latest "in" places travels on the grapevine, and things tends to change fast. Go to the Soleil for an apéritif before it goes out of fashion! For the time being, it's a bar in a working-class neighbourhood with locals of all types: Parisians, Africans in boubous and North Africans. At the end of the day, the big sunny terrace is full of young people from all over Paris who come to relax and drink a (cheap) beer or a Ricard. The kind of place where someone is likely to start playing a guitar.

Les Portes

15, Rue de Charonne 75011.
☎ **01.40.21.70.61.**
M° Bastille.
Open daily 11am-2am; Sun 5pm-2am.

This cosy, intimate little bar is absolutely perfect for a tête-à-tête. Step down into the bar and you'll soon feel at home in this warm and inviting place with its odd bits of furniture and good music; it's ideal for a drink late on a winter afternoon, or for sipping an apéritif while you wait for a table in one of the nearby restaurants. There's a little outdoors terrace with tables in the summer, where you can sit and watch the local talent go by. Good salads at lunchtime.

La Liberté

196, Rue du faubourg Saint-Antoine 75012 Paris.
☎ **01 43 72 11 18.**
M° Faidherbe-Chaligny.
Open daily 9am-2am.

Cabarets and revues

Bring on the dancing girls! If you're looking for a little glitter, the following addresses are for you:

La Belle Époque, 36, Rue des Petits-Champs, 75002, ☎ 01.42.96.33.33.

The sexiest: **Crazy Horse,** 12, Ave George-V, 75008, ☎ 01.47.23.32.32.

A must: **Le Lido,** 116 bis, Ave des Champs-Élysées, 75008, ☎ 01.40.76.56.10.

Drag queens and comedy: **Chez Michou,** 80, Rue des Martyrs, 75018, ☎ 01.42.57.20.37.

A great classic: **Le Paradis Latin,** 28, Rue du Cardinal-Lemoine, 75005, ☎ 01.43.25.28.28.

There was nothing special about this local bistro until a change of management turned it into a great little café. The clientèle has changed too; it's young and trendy, but less pretentious than at the Bastille. There's live music on Saturday nights. Chess and backgammon at your disposal the rest of the time.

Satellit Café
44, Rue de la Folie-Méricourt, 75011.
☎ **01.47.00.48.87.**
M° Oberkampf, Parmentier, Saint-Ambroise.
Mon. to Thurs. 6pm-2am, Fri. and Sat. 6pm to dawn.

Timeless rather than trendy, for anyone over 18 years old. Eighteenth-century musical notation on a terra-cotta background, LP jackets decorating the walls, copper tables and black iron chairs. Rock and flamenco, Cuban or Tibetan music, traditional French songs. Drinks from 35 to 68 francs, and you can dance if you feel like it.

Dance bars

Les Bouchons
19, Rue des Halles, 75001.
☎ **01.42.33.28.73.**
M° Châtelet. Daily noon-3pm, 8pm-1am. Brunch Sat. noon-4pm, Sun noon-5pm.

A bar, half-way between classic and modern with a cosy décor and its own DJ who's ready to play your suggestions. Admission 80 francs, with a first drink, 50 francs for the second drink.

La Casbah
18-20, Rue de la Forge-Royale, 75011.
☎ **01.43.71.71.89.**
M° Ledru-Rollin, Faidherbe-Chaligny.
Daily, bar from 8pm, disco Thurs. and Fri. at 11pm.

Ties are not essential, but there is a bouncer at the door. The decor is Moroccan; the music, acid jazz with an Oriental flavour. Belly dancing at 11pm Fri. and Sat. Admission with drink: 120 francs. Second drink: 50 francs.

Le Moloko
26, Rue Fontaine, 75009.
☎ **01.48.74.50.26.**
M° Pigalle.
Daily 9:30pm-6am.

On the ground floor, there's a juke-box with a choice of 100 CDs for dancing if you want to. There's another bar upstairs, which is open at weekends; it has paintings based on the theme of "woman", a red-velvet décor, and actors or musicians who can use the mini-stage.

Happy hour till 1am, with beer for 15 francs, spirits for 20 francs. At night, beer is 35 francs; spirits, 50 francs.

What's Up

15, Rue Daval, 75011.
☎ 01.48.05.88.33.
M° Bastille.
Daily 8pm-2am.

A gigantic, spacious bar, soft lighting for a late-night atmosphere (starting 11pm). Groove, newjack, soul, acid jazz. What's Up nights on Fridays and Saturdays, with a DJ. Don't wear anything too outrageous. The decor is by a

Late-night dining

Au Pied de Cochon

You can find anything in Paris, including restaurants open 24 hours a day. **L'Alsace aux Halles**, 16, Rue Coquillère, 75001, ☎ 01.42.36.74.24. **Cosmos Café**, 101, Blvd Montparnasse, 75006, ☎ 01.43.26.74.36. **Le Grand Café Capucines**, 4, Blvd des Capucines, 75009, ☎ 01.43.12.19.00. **La Maison d'Alsace**, 39, Ave des Champs Élysées, ☎ 01.53.93.97.00. **Au Pied de Cochon**, 6, Rue Coquillère, 75001, ☎ 01.40.13.77.00. **Pub Saint-Germain**, 17, Rue de l'Ancienne-Comédie,

designer who worked with Starck. Happy hour from 8-10.30pm: 20 to 45 francs; after 10.30pm, 30 to 55 francs. Thursdays, Fridays, and Saturdays, admission (including drink): 50 francs.

Night-clubs

Queen

102, Avenue des Champs-Élysées, 75008.
☎ 01.53.89.08.90.
M° Charles-de-Gaulle-Étoile.
Open every night from midnight.

The most fashionable night-club of the moment, even though it's theoretically a gay club. Every Friday is "Made in Queen" night, with a different international DJ every week. Disco nights on Mondays and shows every evening. Friday, Saturday and Sunday: 100 francs with a drink; 50 francs on Monday, free on other nights. Don't bother arriving before midnight or 1 in the morning. If you only have one night to spare, this is the place to go.

Les Bains

7, Rue du Bourg-l'Abbé, 75003.
☎ 01.48.87.01.80.
M° Étienne Marcel.
Daily 11:30pm to dawn.
Restaurant 10:30pm-1am.

Jonathan Amar designed the baroque decor (red, gold and burgundy) in this temple of the night, where the beautiful people and the happy few mix with visiting stars. If you come with a habitué or have an invitation, you'll have no difficulty getting

in; otherwise it's best to try your luck as a couple. All kinds of music, including world and groove. Admission: 100 francs weekdays, 140 francs Fridays and Saturdays, including drink. Second drink: 100 francs.

Le Bal, Élysée Montmartre

72, Blvd de Rochechouart, 75018. ☎ 01.42.52.76.84.
M° Anvers.
11pm-5am every other Saturday.

A cross between a local hop and a disco, with all kinds of dance music played by the Élysée Montmartre band or the DJ. A mixed crowd of all ages, and plenty of golden oldies. Don't be in too much of a hurry to get in, it's very popular. Admission: 80 francs, drinks from 25 to 40 francs.

Le Balajo

9, Rue de Lappe, 75011.
☎ 01.47.00.07.87.
M° Bastille.
Wed.-Sat. 11:30pm-5:30am; afternoon ballroom dancing Sat. and Sun. 3-6:30pm (entrance: 50 francs).

Pass the hat round, it was the Balajo's 60th birthday in June 96! Zazou-swing on Wednesday nights, rock and Cuban on Thursdays, rock and swing on Fridays and Saturdays. Admission: 100 francs, including drink.

Going out, it's easy !

TICKET +

Tél. : 00 33 1 49 87 50 50
3615 BILLETEL

Theatre / Lives / Opera
Festivals / Sports / Humour
Attraction Parcs / Exhibitions...

This guide was written by **Catherine Synave**, updated by Frédérique Pélissier and Marie-Caroline Dufayet, with the assistance Betty der Andreassian

Translator: **Lisa Davidson**
Copy editor: **Elizabeth Ayre**

This guide was written and researched with the greatest attention to accuracy, yet opening hours may alter, and addresses may change. Please send us your impressions and let us know about your own discoveries. We are always happy to receive letters from our readers.

Guides *Un Grand Week-End*, Hachette Tourisme, 43 quai de Grenelle – 75905 Paris Cedex 15.

Photographic credits

Inside pages
Christian Sarramon: pp. 2 (t.c.), 3 (t.l., c., b.l., b.r.), 8 (t.r., c.l.), 9 (t.r., c.l. background, c.l. foreground), 10 (t.r.), 11 (t.c., c.r., b.r.), 12 (c., b.), 13, 14, 15 (b.l.), 16 (t.r., c.r., b.), 17, 18 (t.r., c.r.), 19 (b.c.), 20, 21, 25 (t.r.), 26 (c.l. c.r.), 27, 31, 32, 34 (c.r., b.l.), 35 (c.l., b.r.), 36 (c.r., b.), 37 (t.c., c.r., b.), 38 (b.l., b.r.), 39, 40 (b.l.), 41, 42 (c.r.), 43 (c.b., b.r.), 44, 45 (t.c., b.l. rights reserved, b.c.), 46, 47 (c.c., b.r.), 48, 49 (c.l., b.r.), 50 (b.l.), 51, 52, 53 (c.l., c.c., b.r.), 54 (c.), 55 (rights reserved), 56, 57, 58, 59 (t.l., c., b.r.), 61, 62, 63, 64, 65 (t.c., c.r., b.r.), 68 (c.b., b.r.), 69, 71 (t., c.r.), 77, 78 (t.l., b.l., b.r.), 79 (c., b.c.), 83 (t.r.), 84 (c.), 85 (c. b.), 88 (t.r., c. foreground and background), 91 (t., c.l.), 92 (b.r.), 93 (c.r., b.l.), 94 (c.r.), 95 (c.r., b.), 100 (c.), 101 (c.t.r., c. b.), 102 (c.b., c.r.), 105, 106 (c., c.l.), 107 (t.r.), 108, 109 (c.l., b.r.), 111 (t.l., t.c., b. g.), 112 (c.l., c.b.), 113 (t.l., b.l.), 120 (c.), 122 (c.r.).
Marc Michiels: pp. 12 (t.), 15 (t.), 83 (c.l., b.r.), 110 (c., c.r., b.), 111 (c.r., b.r.), 112 (t.r., b.r.), 113 (t.r., b.r.), 113 (t.c., c.r., b.r., b.c.).
Peter Tebbitt: pp. 11 (t.r.), 33 (c.l.), 35 (c.l.), 36 (b.l.), 42 (t., b.l. rights reserved), 50 (b.r.), 60 (b.), 65 (c.l.), 68 (c.l.).
I. Rozenbaum/F. Cirou, Photo Alto: pp. 8-9 (b.), 19 (c.l., c.r.), 34 (c.l.), 110 (t.r.), 116.
Pawel Wysocki: 46 (c.l.)
Laurent Parrault: pp. 89 (c.l.), 91 (b.), 92 (t.)
Éric Guillot: p. 59 (t.l.).
Hachette: pp. 10 (b.), 15 (b.), 18 (c.l.), 22 (c.r.), 26 (t.r., b.), 35 (t.r.), 38 (c.l.), 43 (c.l.), 107 (c.).
Rights reserved: pp. 33 (t.l.), 42 (c.r.), 119 (t.c., c.l.), 120 (t.).
© **Orop (Le Procope):** p. 16 (c.l.). **Lenôtre:** p. 18 (b.). **Fauchon:** p. 19 (t.), 109 (t.r.). © **Christian Lacroix:** pp. 22 (t.l., b.c.), 23 (b.r.). **Christian Louboutin:** p. 23 (t.r.). **Vuitton:** pp. 23 (c.r.), 25 (c.l.). © **Chanel/Mademoiselle Chanel par Hoyningen Huene 1935:** p. 24 (c.l.). **Puiforcat/© Arcadia:** p. 24 (c.r.). **Guerlain:** pp. 24 (t.r.), 82 (t.l.). **Hermès/© F. Dumas:** pp. 24 (b.r.), 37 (c.l.). **Prunier:** p. 24 (c.l.). **Bernardaud:** pp. 37 (c.c.), 98 (b.). **Anna Joliet:** p. 40 (c.r.). **Bonpoint:** pp. 45 (c.r.), 93 (b.l.). **Shu Uemura:** p. 47 (t.l.). **Ch. Tortu:** p. 49 (t.c.). **Le Vieux Campeur/© T.-J. Oremusz:** p. 53 (c.r.). **Café Beaubourg:** p. 54 (b.r.). **Opéra Bastille:** p. 65 (c.l.). **Le Pavillon de la Reine:** p. 70 (c.). **Hôtel Caron de Beaumarchais:** p. 70 (c.r.). **Hôtel Saint-Dominique:** p. 71 (b.r.). **Hôtel Franklin Roosevelt:** p. 72. **Hôtel Galileo:** p. 73 (t.l.). **Hôtel Tronchet:** p. 73 (b.l.). **Hôtel Pergolèse:** p. 73 (b.r.). **Le Grand Colbert:** p. 74 (c.l., b.). **Ambassade d'Auvergne:** p. 74 (c.r.). **Brasserie des Musées:** p. 76. **Lapérouse:** p. 78 (t.r.). **Lucas-Carton:** p. 79 (c.l.). **La Closerie des Lilas:** p. 79 (t.l., c.r.). **Fermette Marbeuf/© H. Boutet:** p. 79 (b.r.). **Benneton:** p. 82 (b.l., c.). **Poilâne:** p. 82 (c.r.). **Androuët:** p. 83 (t.l.). **Lolita Lempicka/© F. Dumoulin:** pp. 84 (t.r.), 85 (t.l.). **GAP/© G. Matoso:** p. 84 (c.l.). **Schinichiro Arakawa:** p. 84 (b.l.). **Martin Grant:** p. 85 (c.r.). **Doria Salambo:** p. 85 (b.r.). **Axes et Loisirs:** p. 86 (c.r.). **Anne Fontaine:** p. 86 (b.l.). **Total Éclipse:** p. 86 (b.r.). **Upla:** p. 86 (t.r.). **Big Ben Club:** 86 (t.l.). **Bleu Forêt:** p. 87 (t.l.). **Camper:** p. 87 (t.r., c.). **Mosquitos/© Univers Presse:** 87 (b.). **Lionel Nath:** p. 88 (b.l.). **Timberland:** p. 89 (c., b.). 106 (b.). **Bain Plus:** p. 90 (c.r., b.r.). **Atomica/© J. L Cagnin:** p. 89 (t.c.). **La Cerise sur le Gâteau:** p. 92 (c.l.). **Croissant:** p. 93 (t.l.). **Avant-Scène:** p. 94 (c.l.). **Globe Trotter:** p. 94 (b.r.). **Conceptua:** p. 94 (c.r.). **Agnès Comar:** p. 95 (c.l.). **Laure Japy:** p. 96 (b.). **Bodum/© J. Polony:** p. 96 (t.c.). **À la mine d'argent:** p. 97 (t.l.). **La Tisanière:** p. 97 (c.l.). **La Maison Ivre:** p. 99 (t.l.). **Taïr Mercier:** p. 99 (t.r.). **Paris-Musées:** p. 99 (c., b.). **Artistes et Modèles:** p. 100 (t., b.). **Axis/© V. Grenuillet:** p. 101 (b.l.). **C.F.O.C.:** p. 102 (c.l.). **Galerie Urubamba:** p. 103. **Matins Bleus:** p. 104 (t., c.). **Surcouf:** p. 107 (b.l.). **Olsen Bornholm:** p. 109 (c., b.). **Bateaux parisiens:** p. 117 (t.l.). © **Nicolas Borel:** p. 117 (c.r.). **Salle Pleyel:** p. 117 (c.l.). © **Florian Kleinefenn/Sipa Press:** p. 118 (t.l.). **Le Bar de la Villa/© P. Bogner:** p. 118 (c.). **Flèche d'Or Café:** p. 119 (b.r.). **Lido:** p. 121. **Au Pied de Cochon:** p. 122 (c.l.). **Le Queen:** p. 122 (c., t.).

Front cover
Ch. Sarramon: t.l., c.c., c.r., b.l., b.r. **M. Michiels:** t.r., c.l. **Image Bank / David de Lossy:** c.r. foreground. **Pix / Ling Bill:** t. foreground. **Fotogram-Stone / Chris Craymer:** b. foreground.

Back cover
Ch. Sarramon: t.r.; b.l. **M. Michiels:** c.r. **Rights reserved:** c.l.

Illustrations
Pascal Garnier

Despite the efforts of our editorial staff, and in accordance with established law (Toulouse 14-01-1887), the publisher cannot be held responsible for any errors or omissions which may be in this guide.

Régie exclusive de publicité: Hachette Tourisme – 43, Quai de Grenelle – 75905 Paris Cedex 15. Contact Muriel Bauchau: ☎ 01 43 92 36 82. The publishers are not responsible for the contents of the advertisements in this guide.

© Hachette Livre (Hachette Tourisme), **1998**

Printed in Italy by Litho 800

Dépôt Légal: 6744 – Février 1998 – Collection N°44 – Edition: 01
ISBN: 2.01.242856-8 – 24/2856/3

If you can stay a few more days and you'd like to try something new, this section will give you a large selection of hotels and restaurants, organised by neighbourhood and by price. The list of restaurants also includes a section on foreign cuisine if you have an urge to try Japanese, Lebanese or Indian cuisine. You don't really need to book a table ahead of time (except for the top-notch restaurants). You should, however, book a hotel room several days before you arrive (see p. 66). Hotel and restaurant prices are indicated in French francs. Have a great trip!

AND A FEW MORE DAYS

1st arrondissement

Hôtel de Rouen *
42, Rue Croix-des-Petits-Champs
☎ 01 42 61 38 21
📠 01 42 61 38 21
Double room: 180 to 350

Hôtel du Lion d'Or *
5, Rue de la Sourdière-Hauteur
205, Rue Saint-Honoré
☎ 01 42 60 09 14
📠 01 42 60 09 14
Double room: 270 to 395

2nd arrondissement

Hôtel Tiquetonne *
6, Rue Tiquetone
☎ 01 42 36 94 58
📠 01 42 36 02 94
Double room: 140 to 240

Hôtel Sainte-Marie *
6, Rue de la Ville-Neuve
☎ 01 42 33 21 61
📠 01 42 33 29 24
Double room: 206 to 280

3rd arrondissement

Hôtel des Fontaines
2, Rue des Fontaines-du-Temple
☎ 01 42 72 25 53
Double room: 160 to 200

Grand Hôtel Arts et Métiers
4, Rue Borda
☎ 01 48 87 73 89
📠 01 48 87 66 58
Double room: 200 to 270

Hôtel Paris France **
72, Rue de Tubirgo
☎ 01 42 78 00 04
📠 01 42 71 99 43
Double room: 220 to 350

Hôtel Picard **
26, Rue de Picardie
☎ 01 48 87 53 82
📠 01 48 87 02 56
Double room: 240 to 390

4th arrondissement

Hôtel de la Herse d'Or *
20, Rue Saint-Antoine
☎ 01 48 87 84 09
📠 01 48 87 94 01
Double room: 200 to 280

Hôtel Andrea **
3, Rue Saint-Bon
☎ 01 42 78 43 93
Double room: 210 to 350

Hôtel Sévigné **
2, Rue Malher
☎ 01 42 72 76 17
Double room: 320 to 368

5th arrondissement

Hôtel des Alliés **
20, Rue Berthollet
☎ 01 43 31 47 52
📠 01 45 35 13 92
Double room: 200 to 300

Hôtel Port-Royal *
8, Blvd Port-Royal
☎ 01 43 31 70 06
📠 01 43 31 33 67
Double room: 208 to 310

Hôtel Le Central *
6, Rue Descartes
☎ 01 46 33 57 93
Double room: 210 to 240

Hôtel des Argonautes **
12, Rue de la Huchette
☎ 01 43 54 09 82
📠 01 44 07 18 84
Double room: 250 to 350

6th arrondissement

Hôtel Delhy's *
22, Rue de l'Hirondelle
☎ 01 43 26 58 25
📠 01 43 26 51 06
Double room: 230 to 370

Hôtel des Académies *
15, Rue de la Grande-Chaumière
☎ 01 43 26 66 44
📠 01 43 26 03 72
Double room: 268 to 325

Hôtel Saint-Michel *
17, Rue Gît-le-Cœur
☎ 01 43 26 98 70
Double room: 280 to 340

Hôtel Stanislas **
5, Rue du Montparnasse
☎ 01 45 48 37 05
📠 01 45 44 54 43
Double room: 330 to 350

Hôtel de la Faculté **
1, Rue Racine
☎ 01 43 26 87 13
📠 01 46 34 73 88
Double room: 345

7th arrondissement

Grand Hôtel Lévêque *
29, Rue Cler
☎ 0147 05 49 15
Double room: 230 to 365

Hôtel La Serre **
24 bis, Rue Cler
☎ 01 47 05 52 33
📠 01 40 62 95 66
Double room: 250 to 380

Hôtel Unesco **
37, Ave de la Motte-Piquet
☎ 01 45 51 55 83
📠 01 47 05 77 59
Double room: 280 to 350

Hôtel de la Paix *
19, Rue du Gros-Caillou
☎ 01 45 55 50 04
Double room: 295 to 370

8th arrondissement

Hôtel Bellevue **
46, Rue Pasquier
☎ 01 43 87 50 68.
📠 01 44 70 01 47
Double room: 225 to 360

9th arrondissement

Clauzel **
33, Rue des Martyrs
☎ 01 48 78 12 24
📠 01 48 78 54 36
Double room: 200 to 290

Riviera **
6, Rue de Turgot
☎ 01 48 78 57 24
📠 01 42 81 10 98
Double room: 295

10th arrondissement

Montana **
164, Rue La Fayette
☎ 01 40 35 80 80
📠 01 40 35 08 73
Double room: 250 to 290

Hôtel d'Enghien **
52, Rue d'Enghien
☎ 01 47 70 56 49
📠 01 45 23 04 52
Double room: 250 to 350

11th arrondissement

Grand Hôtel Amelot **
54, Rue Amelot
☎ 01 48 06 15 19
📠 01 48 06 69 77
Double room: 300 to 350

Résidence Voltaire ★★
132, Blvd Voltaire
☎ 01 43 79 39 83
🖷 01 43 79 31 18
Double room: 310 to 340

12th arrondissement

Lux Hôtel ★★
8, Ave Corbéra
☎ 01 43 43 42 84
🖷 01 43 43 14 45
Double room: 250 to 350

Concordia ★★
38, Blvd Diderot
☎ 01 43 43 54 92
🖷 01 43 47 39 50
Double room: 310 to 330

13th arrondissement

Hôtel des Arts ★★
8, Rue Coypel
☎ 01 47 07 76 32
🖷 01 43 31 18 09
Double room: 290 to 360

Grand Hôtel Jeanne d'Arc ★★
43, Blvd Saint-Marcel
☎ 01 47 07 43 17
🖷 01 47 07 87 17
Double room: 295 to 320

14th arrondissement

Celtic ★
15, Rue d'Odessa
☎ 01 43 20 93 53
🖷 01 43 20 66 07
Double room: 230 to 330

Saphir ★★
70, Rue Daguerre
☎ 0143 22 07 02
🖷 01 40 47 67 78
Double room: 330 to 380

15th arrondissement

Royal Lecourbe ★★
286, Rue Lecourbe
☎ 01 45 58 06 05
🖷 01 44 26 33 39
Double room: 180 to 300

Dupleix ★★
4, Rue de Lourmel
☎ 01 45 79 30 12
🖷 01 40 59 84 90
Double room: 260 to 300

16th arrondissement

Exelmans ★★
73, Rue Boileau

☎ 01 42 24 94 66
🖷 01 40 50 37 91
Double room: 280 to 392

17th arrondissement

Hôtel des Batignolles ★★
26-28, Rue des Batignolles
☎ 01 43 87 70 40
🖷 01 44 70 01 04
Double room: 200 to 320

Hôtel des Deux Avenues ★★
38, Rue Poncelet
☎ 01 42 27 44 35
🖷 01 47 63 95 48
Double room: 260 to 390

18th arrondissement

Nouvel Hôtel ★★
86, Rue Myrha
☎ 01 42 64 27 93
🖷 01 42 64 22 39
Double room: 250 to 340

Montmartrois ★★
6 bis, Rue du Chevalier-de-la-Barre
☎ 01 42 62 13 00
🖷 01 42 57 02 33
Double room: 250 to 350

19th arrondissement

Comète ★★
196, Blvd de la Villette
☎ 01 42 08 55 88
🖷 01 42 06 26 35
Double room: 220 to 300

Rhin et Danube ★★
3, Pl. Rhin-et-Danube
☎ 01 42 45 10 13
🖷 01 42 06 88 82
Double room: 300 to 350

20th arrondisement

Dauphine ★★
236, Rue des Pyrénées
☎ 01 43 49 47 66
🖷 01 46 36 05 79
Double room: 250 to 300

Eden ★★
Rue Jean-Baptiste-Dumay
☎ 01 46 36 64 22
🖷 01 46 36 01 00
Double room: 270 to 290

HOTELS UNDER 350 FF

1st arrondissement

Hôtel Louvre-Forum ★★
25, Rue de Bouloi, 75001
☎ 01 42 36 54 19
☏ 01 42 33 66 31
Double room: 350 to 550

Hôtel du Cygne ★★
3, Rue du Cygne
☎ 01 42 60 14 16
☏ 01 42 21 37 02
Double room: 395 to 450

Hôtel Flor-Rivoli ★★
13, Rue des Deux-Boules
☎ 01 42 33 49 60
☏ 01 40 41 05 43
Double room: 420 to 440

Hôtel Saint-Roch ★★
25, Rue Saint-Roch
☎ 01 42 60 17 91
☏ 01 42 61 34 06
Double room: 450 to 540

Timhôtel le Louvre★★
4, Rue Croix-des-Petits-Champs
☎ 01 42 60 34 86
☏ 01 42 60 10 39
Double room: 550

2nd arrondissement

Hôtel Cyrnos ★★★
154, Rue Montmartre
☎ 01 42 33 54 23
☏ 01 45 08 43 47
Double room: 300 to 480

Hôtel Vivienne ★★
40, Rue Vivienne
☎ 01 42 33 13 26
☏ 01 40 41 98 19
Double room: 345 to 450

Hôtel Royal Aboukir ★★★
106, Rue d'Aboukir
☎ 01 42 33 95 04
☏ 01 42 33 05 79
Double room: 390 to 540

Hôtel Marivaux ★★★
10, Rue d'Amboise
☎ 01 42 97 56 58
☏ 01 42 96 56 89
Double room: 480 to 740

Timhôtel la Bourse ★★
3, Rue de la Banque
☎ 01 42 61 53 90
Double room: 550

3rd arrondissement

Hôtel Unic ★★
5, Blvd du Temple
☎ 01 42 72 08 04
☏ 01 42 72 20 33
Double room: 320 to 420

Hôtel de Roubaix ★★
6, Rue de Grenéta
☎ 01 42 72 89 91
☏ 01 42 72 20 33
Double room: 340 to 380

Hôtel du Marais ★★
2 bis, Rue des Commines
☎ 01 48 87 78 27
☏ 01 48 87 09 01
Double room: 360 to 480

Hôtel du Plat d'Étain ★★★
69, Rue Meslay
☎ 01 42 78 04 04
☏ 01 42 74 51 58
Double room: 470 to 520

Hôtel de Saintonge ★★★
16, Rue de Saintonge
☎ 01 42 77 91 13
☏ 01 48 87 76 41
Double room: 490

4th arrondissement

Hôtel Acacias-Hôtel de ville ★★
20, Rue du Temple
☎ 01 48 87 07 70
☏ 01 48 87 17 20
Double room: 400 to 600

Hôtel Seventh Art ★★
20, Rue Saint-Paul
☎ 01 42 77 04 03
☏ 01 42 77 69 10
Double room: 410 to 650

Le Compostelle ★★★
31, Rue du Roi-de-Sicile
☎ 01 42 78 59 99
☏ 01 40 29 05 18
Double room: 450

Hôtel de la Place des Vosges ★★
12, Rue de Birague
☎ 01 42 72 60 46
☏ 01 42 72 02 64
Double room: 450

Hospitel Hôtel Dieu ★★★
1, Pl. du Parvis Notre-Dame
☎ 01 44 32 01 00
☏ 01 44 32 01 16
Double room: 505

5th arrondissement

Hôtel du Brésil ★★
10, Rue Legoff
☎ 01 43 54 76 11
☏ 01 46 33 45 78
Double room: 300 to 410

Hôtel Cluny Sorbonne ★★
8, Rue Victor Cousin
☎ 01 43 54 66 66
☏ 01 43 29 68 07
Double room: 360 to 400

Grand Hôtel Saint-Michel ★★★
19, Rue Cujas, 75005
☎ 01 46 33 33 02
☏ 01 40 36 96 33
Double room: 360 to 500

Hôtel Excelsior ★
20, Rue Cujas
☎ 01 46 34 79 50
☏ 01 43 54 87 10
Double room: 306 to 406

Hôtel Central des Écoles ★★
3, Rue Champollion
☎ 01 46 34 14 20
☏ 01 46 33 74 12
Double room: 400 to 470

Hôtel Cluny Square ★★★
21, Blvd Saint-Michel, 75005
☎ 01 43 54 21 39
☏ 01 44 07 06 71
Double room: 450 to 580

6th arrondissement

Hôtel Saint-Placide ★
6, Rue Saint-Placide
☎ 01 45 48 80 08
☏ 01 45 44 70 32
Double room: 340 to 380

Hôtel Rive Gauche ★★
25, Rue des Saints-Pères
☎ 01 42 60 34 68
☏ 01 42 61 29 78
Double room: 390 to 505

Grand Hôtel des Balcons ★★
3, Rue Casimir Delavigne
☎ 01 46 34 78 50
☏ 01 46 34 06 27
Double room: 440 to 490

Hôtel du Globe et des 4 vents ★★
15, Rue des 4 vents
☎ 01 43 26 35 50
Double room: 450

Hôtel Saint-André-des-Arts ★
66, Rue Saint-André-des-Arts
☎ 01 43 26 96 16
📠 01 43 29 73 34
Double room: 450 to 480

Hôtel Récamier ★★
3 bis, pl. Saint-Sulpice
☎ 01 43 26 04 89.
Double room: 450 to 600

Hôtel du Lys ★★
23, Rue Serpente
☎ 01 43 26 97 57
📠 01 44 07 34 90
Double room: 460

Hôtel Welcome ★★
66, Rue de Seine
☎ 01 46 34 24 80
📠 01 40 46 81 59
Double room: 480 to 515

7th arrondissement

Hôtel Résidence Orsay ★★
93, Rue de Lille, 75007
☎ 01 47 05. 05 27
Double room: 320 to 480

Hôtel Royal-Phare ★★
40, Ave de la Motte-Piquet
☎ 01 47 05 57 30
📠 01 45 51 64 41
Double room: 340 to 400

Mars Hôtel ★★
117, Ave de la Bourdonnais
☎ 01 47 05 42 30
📠 01 47 05 25 81
Double room: 350 to 450

Hôtel Valadon ★★
16, Rue Valadon
☎ 01 47 53 89 85
📠 01 44 18 90 56
Double room: 350 to 550

Hôtel Prince ★★
66, Ave Bosquet
☎ 01 47 05 51 44
📠 01 47 53 06 62
Double room: 350 to 490

Hôtel de Turenne ★★
20, Ave de Tourville
☎ 01 47 0599 92
📠 01 45 56 06 04
Double room: 360 to 400

Hôtel Rapp ★★
8, Ave Rapp
☎ 01 45 51 42 28
📠 01 43 59 50 70
Double room: 380 to 400

Hôtel Palais Bourbon ★★
49, Rue de Bourgogne
☎ 01 44 11 30 70
📠 01 45 55 20 21
Double room: 404 to 545

Hôtel de Nevers ★★
83, Rue du Bac
☎ 01 45 44 61 30
📠 01 42 22 29 47
Double room: 420 to 430

Hôtel Saint-Dominique ★★
62, Rue Saint-Dominique
☎ 01 47 05 51 44
📠 01 47 05 81 28
Double room: 450 to 520

Hôtel Saint-Thomas d'Aquin ★★
3, Rue Pré-aux-Clercs
☎ 01 42 61 01 22
📠 01 42 61 41 43
Double room: 455 to 535

Hôtel Bac Saint-Germain ★★★
66, Rue du Bac
☎ 01 42 22 20 03
📠 01 45 48 52 30
Double room: 490

8th arrondissement

Hôtel d'Argenson ★★
15, Rue d'Argenson
☎ 01 42 65 16 87
📠 01 47 42 02 06
Double room: 330 to 390

Hôtel Océanic ★★
17, Rue de la Pépinière
☎ 01 43 87 40 93
📠 01 45 22 19 45
Double room: 345 to 410

Hôtel Modern-Élysées ★★
9, Rue de Waschington
☎ 01 45 63 27 33
📠 01 45 63 93 49
Double room: 350 to 400

HÔTELS 350 FF TO 500 FF

Hôtel Penthièvre ★★
21, Rue de Penthièvre
☎ 01 43 59 87 63
📠 0145 62 00 76
Double room: 355 to 425

Hôtel de la Paix ★★
22, Rue Roquépine
☎ 01 42 65 14 36
📠 01 42 65 14 36
Double room: 385 to 420

Hôtel Madeleine Opéra ★
12, Rue Greffulhe, 75008
☎ 01 47 42 26 26
📠 01 47 42 89 75
Double room: 400 to 440

Hôtel Marigny ★★
11, Rue de l'Arcade
☎ 01 42 66 42 71
📠 01 47 42 06 76
Double room: 420 to 480

Hôtel Lavoisier Malesherbes ★★
21, Rue Lavoisier
☎ 01 42 65 10 97
📠 01 42 65 02 43
Double room: 430 to 480

Hôtel de l'Ouest ★★
3, Rue du Rocher
☎ 01 43 87 57 49
📠 01 43 87 90 27
Double room: 430 to 510

Timhôtel Sacré Cœur ★★
16, Rue Tholozé
☎ 01 42 55 05 06
📠 01 42 55 00 95
Double room: 440

Hôtel Résidence la Sanguine ★★
6, Rue de Surène
☎ 01 42 65 71 61
📠 01 42 66 96 77
Double room: 460 to 520

Hôtel des Champs-Élysées ★★
2, Rue d'Artois
☎ 01 43 59 11 42
📠 01 45 61 00 61
Double room: 470 to 540

Hôtel Charing Cross ★★
39, Rue Pasquier
☎ 01 43 87 41 04
📠 01 42 93 70 45
Double room: 470 to 485

Hôtel New-Orient ★★
16, Rue de Constantinople
☎ 01 45 22 21 64
📠 01 42 93 83 23
Double room: 470 to 590

Hôtel Amina ★★★
4, Rue d'Artois
☎ 01 43 59 03 19
📠 01 45 62 03 79
Double room: 490 to 540

Royal Hôtel Champs-Élysées ★★★
7, Rue du Colisée
☎ 01 43 59 32 40
📠 01 43 59 06 19
Double room: 500 to 550

9th arrondissement

Relais du Pré ★★★
16, Rue Pierre-Sémard
☎ 01 42 85 19 59
📠 01 42 85 70 59
Double room: 490 to 515

Hôtel de la Havane ★★
44, Rue de Trévise
☎ 01 47 70 79 12
📠 01 47 70 79 12
Double room: 376 to 476

10th arrondissement

Alane ★★★
72, Blvd Magenta
☎ 01 40 35 83 30
📠 01 46 07 44 03
Double room: 350 to 450

Metropol ★★★
98, Rue de Maubeuge
☎ 01 45 26 83 90
📠 01 48 78 18 81
Double room: 374 to 450

11th arrondissement

Aquarelle ★★
38, Blvd du Temple
☎ 01 48 05 79 76
📠 01 48 05 58 28
Double room: 360 to 400

Beauséjour ★★★
1, Rue de la Fontaine-au-Roi
☎ 01 43 57 34 01
📠 01 48 05 70 17
Double room: 380 to 510

12th arrondissement

Amadeus ★★
39, Rue Claude-Tillier
☎ 01 43 48 53 48
📠 01 43 48 56 13
Double room: 380 to 400

Aurore ★★★
13, Rue Traversière
☎ 01 43 43 54 12
📠 01 43 43 53 20
Double room: 470 to 530

13th arrondissement

Résidence les Gobelins
9, Rue des Gobelins
☎ 01 47 07 26 90
📠 01 43 31 44 05
Double room: 380 to 455

Équinoxe ★★★
40, Rue le Brun
☎ 001 43 37 56 56
📠 01 45 35 52 42
Double room: 395

14th arrondissement

Delambre ★★
35, Rue Delambre
☎ 01 43 20 66 31
📠 01 45 38 91 76
Double room: 380 to 470

Odessa ★★
28, Rue d'Odessa
☎ 01 43 20 64 78
📠 01 42 79 9071
Double room: 395 to 450

15th arrondissement

Avenir ★★
373, Rue de Vaugirard
☎ 01 45 32 90 14
📠 01 45 32 14 53
Double room: 400 to 460

Alize Grenelle ★★★
87, Ave Émile-Zola
☎ 01 45 78 08 22
📠 01 40 59 03 06
Double room: 430 to 510

16th arrondissement

Villa Caroline ★★★
85, Rue de la Pompe
☎ 01 45 04 67 38
Double room: 350 to 400

Au Palais de Chaillot ★★
35, Ave Raymond-Poincaré
☎ 01 53 70 09 09
📠 01 53 70 09 08
Double room: 500 to 550

17th arrondissement

Ouest ★★
165, Rue de Rome
☎ 01 42 27 50 29
🖷 01 42 27 27 40
Double room: 326 to 426

18th arrondissement

Damrémont ★★
110, Rue Damrémont
☎ 01 42 64 25 75
🖷 01 46 06 74 64
Double room: 350 to 490

Regny's Montmarte ★★
18, Pl. des Abesses
☎ 01 42 54 45 21
🖷 01 42 23 76 69
Double room: 435 to 455

19th arrondissement

Hôtel du parc des Buttes-Chaumont ★★
1, Pl. Armand-Carrel
☎ 01 42 08 08 37
🖷 01 42 45 66 91
Double room: 360 to 450

Hôtel des Buttes Chaumont ★★
4, Ave Secrétan
☎ 01 42 45 33 81
🖷 01 42 45 60 40
Double room: 370

20th arrondisement

Palma ★★
77, Ave Gambetta
☎ 01 46 36 13 65
🖷 01 46 36 03 27
Double room: 355 to 400

Armstrong ★★
36, Rue de la Croix-Saint-Simon
☎ 01 43 70 53 65
🖷 01 43 70 63 31
Double room: 490

HOTELS 350 FF TO 500 FF

FRENCH CUISINE

Au Diable des Lombards
64, Rue des Lombards
☎ 01 42 33 81 84
📠 01 42 33 73 99
À la carte 80FF, menu 60-125FF

Le Sundeck
8, Pl. Marguerite-de-Navarre
☎ 01 42 21 31 31
📠 01 42 21 32 72
À la carte 140FF, menu 90-130FF

Le Charles Baudelaire
8, Rue Duphot
☎ 01 42 60 34 12
📠 01 47 03 95 20
À la carte 140FF, menu 95-180FF

Le Grand Louvre
Pyramide du Louvre
☎ 01 40 20 53 20
📠 01 42 86 04 63
À la carte 210FF, menu 180FF

L'Échelle
7, Rue de l'Échelle
☎ 01 42 86 97 69
À la carte 220FF, menu 150FF

BRASSERIE

Brasserie du Louvre
Pl. du Palais-Royal
☎ 01 42 96 27 98
📠 01 44 58 38 01
À la carte 200FF, menu 100-145FF

Café de l'Univers
159, Rue Saint-Honoré
☎ 01 42 60 31 57
📠 01 42 61 36 33
À la carte 200FF, menu 120-180FF

Au Pied de Cochon
6, Rue Coquillère
☎ 01 40 13 77 00
📠 01 40 13 77 09
À la carte 250FF, menu 180FF

BISTROT

Le Panorama
14, Quai du Louvre
☎ 01 42 33 32 37
📠 01 42 33 83 72
À la carte 120FF, menu 80-150FF

Lescure
7, Rue de Mondovi
☎ 01 42 60 18 91
À la carte 150FF, menu 100FF

FRENCH CUISINE

Les Deux Ducs
95, Rue de Richelieu
☎ 01 42 96 83 87
📠 01 40 15 08 50
À la carte 100FF, menu 70-80FF

Aux Lyonnais
32, Rue Saint-Marc
☎ 01 42 96 65 04
📠 01 42 97 42 95
À la carte 150FF

BRASSERIE

Chez Clément
17, Blvd des Capucines
☎ 01 53 43 82 00
📠 01 53 43 82 09
À la carte 160FF, menu 90-130FF

Le Vaudeville
29, Rue Vivienne
☎ 01 40 20 04 62
📠 01 49 27 08 78
À la carte 200FF, menu 130-170FF

BISTROT

Bourse Batifol
157, Rue Montmartre
☎ 01 42 36 68 40
📠 01 40 28 43 21
À la carte 115FF

Le Bistrot de Jeannette
14, Rue Favart
☎ 01 42 96 36 89
📠 01 47 03 97 31
À la carte 150FF, menu 100170FF

FRENCH CUISINE

Au Marais Gourmand
26, Rue Charlot
☎ 01 48 87 63 08
À la carte 110FF, menu 70-120FF

La Guirlande de Julie
25, Pl. des Vosges
☎ 01 48 87 94 07
À la carte 165FF, menu 65-165FF

Auberge Nicolas Flamel
51, Rue de Montmorency
☎ 01 42 71 77 78
À la carte 170FF, menu 70-300FF

Le Bar à Huître
33, Blvd Beaumarchais
☎ 01 48 87 98 92
📠 01 48 87 04 42
À la carte 200-240FF, menu 130-200FF

Ambassade d'Auvergne
24, Rue du Grenier-Saint-Lazare
☎ 01 42 72 31 22
📠 01 42 78 85 47
À la carte 230FF, menu 170FF

FRENCH CUISINE

Au Rendez-Vous des Amis
10, Rue Sainte-Croix-de-la-Bretonnerie
☎ 01 42 72 05 99
À la carte 150FF, menu 100FF

Amadeo
19, Rue François-Miron
☎ 01 48 87 01 02
📠 01 42 76 08 38
À la carte 165FF, menu 85-165FF

Nos Ancêtres les Gaulois
39, Rue Saint-Louis-en-l'Ile
☎ 01 46 33 66 12
📠 01 43 25 28 64
Menu 190FF

Auberge de la Reine Blanche
30, Rue Saint-Louis-en-l'Ile
☎ 01 46 33 07 87
📠 01 43 29 55 73
À la carte 250FF, menu 90-140FF

BRASSERIE

Les Rivolines
46, Rue de Rivoli
☎ 01 42 78 65 87
Menu 50-120FF

Bofinger
5-7, Rue de la Bastille
☎ 01 42 72 87 82
📠 01 42 72 97 68
À la carte 200-250FF, menu 170FF

BISTROT

Le Trumilou
84, Quai de l'Hôtel-de-Ville
☎ 01 42 77 63 98
☏ 01 48 04 91 89
À la carte 130FF, menu 65-80FF

Bistrot Bofinger
6, Rue de la Bastille
☎ 01 42 72 05 23
☏ 01 42 72 07 68
Menu 90-130FF

À l'Impasse
4, Imp. Guémenée
☎ 01 42 72 08 45
À la carte 180FF, menu 140FF

5th arrondissement

FRENCH CUISINE

La Cochonnaille
21, Rue de la Harpe
☎ 01 46 33 96 81
☏ 01 40 51 77 36
À la carte 120FF, menu 70-110FF

La Parcheminerie
31, Rue de la Parcheminerie
☎ 01 46 33 65 12
☏ 01 40 51 77 36
Menu 140-200FF

Alexandre
24, Rue de la Parcheminerie
☎ 01 43 26 49 66
À la carte 220FF, menu 90FF

Le Petit Navire
14, Rue des Fossés-Saint-Bernard
☎ 01 43 54 22 52
À la carte 250FF, menu 150FF

BRASSERIE

La Rôtisserie du Beaujolais
19, quai de la Tournelle
☎ 01 43 54 17 47
☏ 01 44 07 12 04
À la carte 230FF

FAST FOOD

Salon des Trois Collèges
16, Rue Cujas
☎ 01 43 54 67 30

☎ 01 46 34 02 99
À la carte 60FF, menu 50FF

La Cour aux Crêpes
27, Rue Galande
☎ 01 43 25 45 00
À la carte 65-80FF, menu 50FF

6th arrondissement

FRENCH CUISINE

Comptoir des Sports
3, Rue Hautefeuille
☎ 01 43 54 35 46
☏ 01 46 33 95 01
À la carte 90FF, menu 100-150FF

Côté Seine
45, Quai des Grands-Augustins
☎ 01 43 54 49 73
☏ 01 43 26 43 80
À la carte 130-180FF, menu 130-150FF

La Table du Périgord
13, Rue de Mézières
☎ 01 45 48 30 38
À la carte 150FF, menu 80-160FF

Jardin Saint-Germain
14, Rue du Dragon
☎ 01 45 44 72 82
☏ 01 42 84 28 66
À la carte 200FF, menu 70-100FF

Au Petit Prince
3, Rue Monsieur-le-Prince
☎ 01 43 29 74 92
À la carte 220FF, menu 100-140FF

BRASSERIE

Brasserie Saint-Benoît
26, Rue Saint-Benoît
☎ 01 45 48 29 66
☏ 01 45 44 50 07
À la carte 150FF, menu 70-130FF

Chope d'Alsace
4, carr. de l'Odéon
☎ 01 43 26 67 76
☏ 01 46 34 58 30
À la carte 150FF, menu 120-170FF

Pub Saint-Germain
17, Rue de l'Ancienne-Comédie
☎ 01 43 29 38 70
☏ 01 40 51 72 25
À la carte 200FF, menu 50-160FF

La Grosse Horloge
22, Rue Saint-Benoît

RESTAURANTS

☎ 01 42 22 22 63
🅕 01 45 44 18 65
À la carte 200FF, menu 100FF

BISTROT

Restaurant des Beaux-Arts
11, Rue Bonaparte
☎ 01 43 26 92 64
🅕 01 43 29 70 44
À la carte 100FF, menu 85FF

Restaurant Gît-le-Cœur
14, Rue Gît-le-Cœur
☎ 01 46 33 02 06
🅕 01 43 29 98 82
À la carte 150FF, menu 90-130FF

Aux Charpentiers
10, Rue Mabillon
☎ 01 43 26 30 05
🅕 01 46 33 07 98
À la carte 200FF, menu 120-153FF

RESTAURATION RAPIDE

La Bolée
25, Rue Servandoni
☎ 01 46 34 17 68
À la carte 50-70FF

7th arrondissement

FRENCH CUISINE

Le Chevert
34, Rue Chevert
☎ 01 47 05 51 09
À la carte 100-150FF, menu 100-160FF

Chez l'Ami Jean
27, Rue Malar
☎ 01 47 05 86 89
🅕 01 45 55 71 42
À la carte 150-180FF, menu 100FF

Les Ministères
30, Rue du Bac
☎ 01 42 61 22 37
🅕 01 42 86 87 33
À la carte 160FF, menu 90-170 F

Thoumieux
79, Rue Saint-Dominique
☎ 01 47 05 49 75
🅕 01 47 05 36 96
À la carte 180FF, menu 90-160FF

Du Côté 7e
29, Rue Surcouf

☎ 01 47 05 81 65
Menu 180FF

Nuit de Saint-Jean
29, Rue Surcouf
☎ 01 45 51 61 49
🅕 01 47 05 36 40
À la carte 180FF, menu 120FF

Chez Françoise
2, Rue Robert-Esnault-Pelterie
☎ 01 47 05 49 03
🅕 01 45 51 96 20
À la carte 200-250FF, menu 120-180FF

BRASSERIE

Le Bourbon
1, Pl. du Palais-Bourbon
☎ 01 45 51 58 27
🅕 01 45 51 06 25
À la carte 150FF, menu 90-180FF

Altitude 95
Eiffel Tower, 1st floor
☎ 01 45 55 00 21
🅕 01 47 05 94 40
À la carte 250FF, menu 100-240FF

BISTROT

La Serre
29, Rue de l'Exposition
☎ 01 45 55 20 96
🅕 01 45 55 06 65
À la carte 150FF

À la Petite Chaise
36, Rue de Grenelle
☎ 01 42 22 13 35
🅕 01 42 22 33 84
À la carte 180FF, menu 110-150FF

8th arrondissement

FRENCH CUISINE

Le Matignon
76/78, Ave des Champs-Élysées
☎ 01 53 83 78 27
🅕 01 45 63 02 84
À la carte 100FF, menu 95-200FF

Le Cellier
11, Rue d'Amsterdam
☎ 01 53 42 17 89
🅕 01 42 93 79 12
À la carte 170FF, menu 100-190FF

Le Val d'Isère à Paris
2, Rue de Berri
☎ 01 43 59 12 66

🅕 01 45 61 25 38
À la carte 200FF, menu 150-180FF

Le Grand Corona
3, Pl. de l'Alma
☎ 01 47 23 49 70
🅕 01 47 20 70 53
À la carte 200-300FF, menu 138-250FF

La Ferme des Mathurins
17, Rue Vignon
☎ 01 42 66 46 39
🅕 01 42 66 00 27
À la carte 250FF, menu 150-210 FF

La Fermette Marbeuf 1900
5, Rue Marbeuf
☎ 01 53 23 08 00
🅕 01 53 23 08 09
À la carte 300FF, menu 180FF

La Luna
69, Rue du Rocher
☎ 01 42 93 77 61
🅕 01 40 08 02 44
À la carte 350-450FF

BRASSERIE

Café George V
120, Ave des Champs-Élysées
☎ 01 45 62 33 51
🅕 01 45 63 04 61
À la carte 110-120FF, menu 80-160FF

Café Leffe
150, Ave des Champs-Élysées
☎ 01 43 59 87 54
🅕 01 43 59 68 27
À la carte 120FF, menu 60-130FF

Pub Renault
53, Ave des Champs-Élysées
☎ 01 42 25 28 17
🅕 01 42 89 04 93
À la carte 150FF, menu 60-100FF

Bœuf sur le Toit
34, Rue du Colisée
☎ 01 53 93 65 55
🅕 01 45 63 45 40
À la carte 250FF, menu 120-170FF

Brasserie Mollard
115, Rue Saint-Lazare
☎ 01 43 87 50 22
🅕 01 43 87 84 17
À la carte 200FF, menu 130-185FF

BISTROT

Xavier
89, Blvd de Courcelles
☎ 01 43 80 78 22
À la carte 120FF, menu 85-110FF

Le Table du Marché
14, Rue de Marignan
☎ 01 40 76 34 44
🖷 01 40 76 34 10
À la carte 200FF, menu 160FF

9th arrondissement

FRENCH CUISINE

Le Viking
55, Rue du Faubourg-Montmartre
☎ 01 42 80 39 02
🖷 01 40 16 15 37
À la carte 150FF, menu 65-95FF

La Cloche d'Or
3, Rue Mansart
☎ 01 48 74 48 88
🖷 01 40 16 40 99
À la carte 170FF, menu 80-110FF

Les Diables au Thym
35, Rue Bergère
☎ 01 47 70 77 09
À la carte 250FF, menu 90-120FF

BRASSERIE

Café Flo Printemps
64, Blvd Haussmann
☎ 01 42 82 55 82
🖷 01 45 26 31 24
À la carte 110FF, menu 60-140FF

La Taverne Kronenbourg
24, Blvd des Italiens
☎ 01 47 70 16 64
🖷 01 42 47 13 91
À la carte 200FF, menu 140FF

10th arrondissement

FRENCH CUISINE

Le Saulnier
39, Blvd de Strasbourg
☎ 01 47 70 08 31
🖷 01 42 47 05 48
À la carte 60FF, menu 80-135FF

Les Étoiles
61, Rue du Château-d'Eau
☎ 01 47 70 60 56

🖷 01 44 83 96 44
À la carte 100FF

Le Trait d'Union
13, Rue des Deux-Gares
☎ 01 42 09 72 99
🖷 01 42 09 72 80
À la carte 150FF, menu 80-110FF

BRASSERIE

Le P'tit Quinquin
150, Rue La Fayette
☎ 01 40 34 74 64
🖷 01 40 34 61 31
À la carte 90FF, menu 60-90FF

Au Petit Duc
14-16, Blvd Bonne-Nouvelle
☎ 01 47 70 30 46
🖷 01 48 24 01 16
À la carte 90FF, menu 70-100FF

BISTROT

Le Chansonnier
14, Rue Eugène-Varlin
☎ 01 42 09 40 58
🖷 01 40 38 06 78
À la carte 160FF, menu 90-180FF

11th arrondissement

FRENCH CUISINE

Le Relais du Massif Central
16, Rue Daval
☎ 01 47 00 46 55
À la carte 150FF, menu 95-120FF

Les 5 Points Cardinaux
14, Rue Jean-Macé
☎ 01 43 71 47 22
À la carte 150FF, menu 100FF

BRASSERIE

Le Bastide
74, Rue Amelot
☎ 01 40 21 20 00
🖷 01 47 00 82 40
À la carte 130FF, menu 110FF

12th arrondissement

FRENCH CUISINE

À la Biche au Bois
45, Ave Ledru-Rollin
☎ 01 43 43 34 38
À la carte 145FF, menu 100-120FF

RESTAURANTS

La Flambée
4, Rue Taine
☎ 01 43 43 21 80
À la carte 200FF, menu 125-200FF

Les Fleurs du Berry
197, Ave Daumesnil
☎ 01 43 43 24 61
À la carte 200FF, menu 145-165FF

BRASSERIE

La Tour de Lyon
1, Rue de Lyon
☎ 01 43 43 88 30
📠 01 43 43 89 80
À la carte 180FF, menu 140-190FF

Brasserie l'Européen
21 bis, Blvd Diderot
☎ 01 43 43 99 70
📠 01 43 07 26 51
À la carte 200FF, menu 90-150FF

13th arrondissement

BRASSERIE

Le Rozes
30, Ave d'Italie ou 19, Rue Bobillot — Centre Italie 2
☎ 01 43 80 66 34
📠 01 45 80 73 22
À la carte 150FF, menu 80-180FF

Le Grenadier
Buffet Gare Austerlitz
55, Quai d'Austerlitz
☎ 01 45 84 38 55
📠 01 45 70 86 32
À la carte 180FF, menu 140FF

BISTROT

Chez Françoise
12, Rue de la Butte-aux-Cailles
☎ 01 45 80 12 02
📠 01 45 65 13 67
À la carte 220FF, menu 70-90FF

14th arrondissement

RESTAURATION CLASSIQUE

Les Gourmands
101, Rue de l'Ouest
☎ 01 45 41 40 70.
Menu 100-140FF

La Panetière
9, Rue Maison-Dieu
☎ 01 43 22 04 02
Menu 100FF

Au Moulin Vert
34 bis, Rue des Plantes
☎ 01 45 39 31 31
À la carte 155FF, menu 90-180FF

BRASSERIE

La Coupole
102, Blvd du Montparnasse
☎ 01 43 20 14 20
📠 01 43 35 46 14
À la carte 170FF, menu 90-120FF

Le Bar à Huître
112, Blvd du Montparnasse
☎ 01 43 20 71 01
À la carte 230FF, menu 100-200FF

BISTROT

Bergamote
1, Rue Niepce
☎ 01 43 22 79 47
Menu 60FF, 120FF

La Cagouille
10, Pl. Constantin-Brancusi
☎ 01 43 22 09 01
📠 01 45 38 57 29
À la carte 220FF, menu 150-250FF

15th arrondissement

FRENCH CUISINE

La Cantine des Photographes
76, Rue de la Procession
☎ 01 40 61 09 91
Menu 70-85FF

Bermuda Onion
16, Rue de Linois — Centre Beaugrenelle
☎ 01 45 75 11 11
À la carte 200FF

BRASSERIE

Chez Clément
407, Rue de Vaugirard
☎ 01 53 68 94 00
À la carte 150FF, menu 130FF

BISTROT

Le Volant
13, Rue Béatrix-Dussane
☎ 01 45 75 27 67
Menu 130FF

Chez Pierre
117, Rue de Vaugirard

☎ 01 47 34 96 12
À la carte 180FF, menu 100-150FF

FAST FOOD

Self la Motte-Picquet
63, Ave de la Motte-Picquet
☎ 01 43 06 90 86
📠 01 47 34 49 02
À la carte 85-100FF, menu 80FF

16th arrondissement

FRENCH CUISINE

Zebra Square
3, Pl. Clément-Ader
☎ 01 44 14 91 91
📠 01 45 20 46 41
À la carte 170FF, menu 200FF

Le Presbourg
3, Ave de la Grande-Armée
☎ 01 45 00 24 77
📠 01 45 00 95 50
À la carte 195FF, menu 100-120FF

L'Orée du Bois
1, Allée de Longchamp — Bois de Boulogne
☎ 01 40 67 92 50
À la carte 220FF, menu 170FF

BRASSERIE

Café Le Malakoff
6, Pl. du Trocadéro
☎ 01 45 53 75 27
À la carte 100FF, menu 65FF

Arc de Triomphe
73, Ave Marceau
☎ 01 47 20 72 04
À la carte 100FF, menu 80-120FF

BISTROT

Auberge du Bonheur
Bois de Boulogne
☎ 01 42 24 10 17
À la carte 180-200FF, menu 160FF

17th arrondissement

RESTAURATION CLASSIQUE

Café Arlequin
81, Blvd Gouvion-Saint-Cyr
☎ 01 40 68 30 85
À la carte 160FF

BRASSERIE

Chez Clément Maillot
99, Blvd Gouvion-Saint-Cyr
☎ 01 45 72 93 00
*À la carte 100-120FF,
menu 130FF*

Baumann Ternes
64, Ave des Ternes
☎ 01 45 74 16 66
🅕 01 45 72 44 32
*À la carte 190FF,
menu 120-180FF*

Le Ballon des Ternes
103, Ave des Ternes
☎ 01 45 74 17 98
🅕 01 45 72 18 84
À la carte 200-250FF

Le Congrès Maillot
80, Ave de la Grande-Armée
☎ 01 45 74 17 24
🅕 01 45 72 39 80
À la carte 250FF, menu 130FF

BISTROT

L'Espace Dégustation
39, Rue Laugier
☎ 01 47 54 05 02
À la carte 120FF, menu 80FF

FAST FOOD

Valerine
17, Rue de l'Étoile
☎ 01 44 09 01 33
🅕 01 44 09 01 43
À la carte 30FF, menu 40-50FF

18th arrondissement

FRENCH CUISINE

Le Va et Vient du Nord
55, Rue Ordener
☎ 01 42 52 25 21
*À la carte 180FF,
menu 60-100FF*

Bistrot de Montmarte
7, Ave Rachel
☎ 01 42 93 90 04
🅕 01 42 94 88 42
À la carte 180FF, menu 100FF

Butte en Vigne
5, Rue Poulbot, Pl. du Tertre

☎ 01 46 06 91 96
🅕 01 42 64 16 40
*À la carte 200FF,
menu 100-150FF*

BRASSERIE

La Crémaillère
15, Pl. du Tertre
☎ 01 46 06 58 59
🅕 01 42 64 08 57
*À la carte 200FF,
menu 70-160FF*

La Bohème du Tertre
2, Pl. du Tertre
☎ 01 46 06 51 69
🅕 01 42 62 41 53
*À la carte 200FF,
menu 150-200FF*

Wepler
14, Pl. de Clichy
☎ 01 45 22 53 29
🅕 01 44 70 07 50
*À la carte 270FF,
menu 105-150FF*

19th arrondissement

FRENCH CUISINE

Pavillon du Lac
Parc des Buttes-Chaumont
☎ 01 42 02 08 97
🅕 01 42 02 54 73
*À la carte 250FF,
menu 100-230FF*

20th arrondissement

FRENCH CUISINE

Le Zéphyr
1, Rue du Jourdain
☎ 01 46 36 65 81
Menu 150FF

Les Allobroges
71, Rue des Grands-Champs
☎ 01 43 73 40 00
*À la carte 200FF,
menu 90-170FF*

BISTROT

Le Vieux Belleville
12, Rue des Envierges
☎ 01 44 62 92 66
*À la carte 120FF,
menu 55-65FF*

RESTAURANTS

African

N'zadette M'Foua
152, Rue du Château,
75014
☎ 01 43 22 00 16
À la carte 45-120FF, menu 60FF

Kaï Savane
10, Rue Marie-Stuart,
75002
☎ 01 40 28 00 94
*À la carte 100-150FF,
menu 70-130FF*

SÉNÉGAL

Chez Aïda
48, Rue Polonceau,
75018
☎ 01 42 58 26 20
À la carte 70-120FF

Paris-Dakar
95, Rue du Faubourg-
Saint-Martin, 75010
☎ 01 42 08 16 64
☏ 01 42 03 11 25
*À la carte 70-170FF,
menu 70-160 FF*

NORTH AFRICAN

Au Petit Cahoua
39, Blvd Saint-Marcel,
75005
☎ 01 47 07 24 42
*À la carte 75-200FF,
menu 95-140FF*

Chez Omar
47, Rue de Bretagne,
75003
☎ 01 42 72 36 26
À la carte 95-170FF

La Colline des Potiers
271, Rue du Faubourg-
Saint-Antoine, 75011
☎ 01 43 73 45 98
À la carte 130FF, menu 100FF

American

Chicago Meatpackers
8, Rue Coquillière, 75001
☎ 01 40 28 02 33
☏ 01 40 41 95 84
*À la carte 90-200FF,
menu 80FF*

American Dream
21, Rue Daunou, 75002
☎ 01 42 60 99 89
☏ 01 42 61 12 27
À la carte 100FF

Hard Rock Café
14, Blvd Montmartre,
75009
☎ 01 42 46 10 00
☏ 01 42 46 49 70
À la carte 120FF, menu 75-85FF

MEXICAN

Ay! Caramba
59, Rue de Mouzaïa,
75019
☎ 01 42 41 76 30
☏ 01 42 41 50 34
À la carte 50-150FF

Taco Loco
116, Rue Amelot, 75011
☎ 01 43 57 90 24
À la carte 100FF

TEXAN

The Studio
41, Rue du Temple,
75004
☎ 01 42 74 10 38
À la carte 150FF

Asian

**Nouveau Orient
Express**
72, Rue des Gravilliers,
75003
☎ 01 42 77 23 76
À la carte 80-200FF, menu 50FF

CAMBODIAN

Sinago
17, Rue de Maubeuge,
75009
☎ 01 48 78 11 14
À la carte 50-200FF, menu 55FF

CHINESE

Song Hoat
7, Blvd de la Villette,
75010
☎ 01 42 45 44 99
☏ 01 48 03 21 59
À la carte 30-120FF

Le Bambou Royal
8, Rue Troyon, 75017
☎ 01 43 80 86 06
*À la carte 100-250FF,
menu 70-100FF*

**Auberge
des Trois Bonheurs**
280, Rue Saint-Honoré,
75001
☎ 01 42 60 43 24
À la carte 120FF, menu 110-140FF

Dragons Élysées
11, Rue de Berri, 75008
☎ 01 42 89 85 10
☏ 01 45 63 04 97
À la carte 200FF, menu 75-200FF

Chez Vong
27, Rue du Colisée, 75008
☎ 01 43 59 77 12
☏ 01 43 59 59 27
À la carte 250FF

Le Grand Chinois
6, Ave de New York,
75016
☎ 47 23 98 21
☏ 47 23 99 58
À la carte 250FF, menu 120-150FF

THAI

Krung Thep
93, Rue Julien-Lacroix,
75020
☎ 01 43 66 83 74
À la carte 70-200FF

Chieng Mai
12, Frédéric-Sauton, 75005
☎ 01 43 25 45 45
À la carte 200FF, menu 160FF

VIETNAMESE

Bi Da Saïgon
44, Ave d'Ivry, 75013
☎ 01 45 84 04 85
À la carte 35-45FF

Le Moï
5, Rue Daunou, 75002
☎ 01 47 03 92 05
À la carte 90-250FF, menu 80FF

Da Lat
120, Rue du Faubourg-
de-Temple, 75011
☎ 01 43 38 22 72
À la carte 100FF, menu 70FF

Vu Lan-Phuong
82, Rue Baudricourt,
75013
☎ 01 45 85 20 70
À la carte 90-150FF, menu 60FF

Lac Hong
67, Rue Lauriston, 75016
☎ 47 55 87 17
À la carte 200FF, menu 90FF

Greek

Apollon
24, Rue Jean-Nicot, 75007
☎ 01 45 55 68 47
À la carte 80-200FF, menu 130FF

Calypso
10, Rue Guisarde, 75006
☎ 01 43 54 97 86
*Á la carte 90-180FF,
menu 80-100FF*

La Crête
85, Rue Mouffetard,
75005
☎ 01 43 31 30 47
Á la carte 130FF, menu 60-85FF

Leonidas
6, Rue de La Michodière,
75002
☎ 01 47 42 78 71
Á la carte 140FF, menu 70-80FF

Maharajah
72, Blvd Saint-Germain,
75005
☎ 01 43 54 26 07
☎ 01 40 46 08 18
Á la carte 60-200FF, menu 60-70FF

Joyti
148, Rue de Vaugirard,
75015
☎ 01 47 83 45 45
☎ 01 45 67 15 93
Carte, 70-200FF, menu 50-130FF

Djakarta Bali
9, Rue de Vauvilliers,
75001
☎ 01 45 08 83 11
*Á la carte 80-200FF,
menu 90-240FF*

Toulsi
30, Ave de Versailles,
75016
☎ 01 45 24 34 98
Á la carte 160FF, menu 120-220FF

Annapurna
32, Rue de Berri, 75008
☎ 01 45 63 91 62
Á la carte 200FF

Vishnou
13, Rue du Commandant-
René-Mouchotte, 75014
☎ 01 45 38 92 93
Á la carte 200FF, menu 220-230FF

Ravi
50, Rue de Verneuil,
75007
☎ 01 42 61 17 28
Á la carte 260FF

Italian

La Mamma
46, Rue Vavin, 75006
☎ 01 46 33 17 92
Á la carte 70-150FF, menu 50FF

La Tavola
10 Rue de la Roquette,
75011
☎ 01 47 00 01 95
Á la carte 80FF, menu 60-80FF

Pizzoletto
166, Blvd Masséna, 75013
☎ 01 44 24 92 22
☎ 01 44 24 97 64
Á la carte 100FF, menu 70FF

Pizza Sarno
31, Rue de la Harpe,
75005
☎ 01 43 29 58 03
Á la carte 100FF, menu 70-90FF

Del Papa
233 bis, Rue du Faubourg-
Saint-Honoré, 75008
☎ 01 47 63 30 98
Á la carte 100-250FF

Villa Medicis, chez Napoli
11 bis, Rue Saint-Placide,
75006
☎ 01 42 22 51 96
Á la carte 180FF, menu 90-115FF

Il Cortile
37, Rue Cambron, 75001
☎ 01 44 58 45 67
Á la carte 250FF, menu 195FF

La Barcarola
275, Rue du Faubourg-
Saint-Antoine, 75011
☎ 01 43 72 24 76
Á la carte 250FF, menu 170FF

Il Ristorante San Felice
39, Rue des
Entrepeneurs, 75015
☎ 01 45 77 93 48
Á la carte 250FF, menu 220FF

Conti
72, Rue Lauriston, 75016
☎ 01 47 27 74 67
Á la carte 300FF, menu 200FF

La Tour de Pise
16, Rue Letort, 75018
☎ 01 42 57 33 74
*Á la carte 80-220FF,
menu 70-100FF*

FOREIGN CUISINE

Japanese

Taki Tang
52, Rue Godefroy-
Cavaignac, 75011
☎ 01 43 67 08 39
À la carte 50-120FF,
menu 50-100FF

Foujita
41, Rue Saint-Roch,
75001
☎ 01 42 61 42 93
À la carte 80-170FF,
menu 70-150FF

Ayamé
10, Rue Rennequin,
75017
☎ 01 42 27 98 00
À la carte 80-200FF,
menu 59-118FF

Sanshiro
45, Rue Richelieu, 75001
☎ 01 42 86 00 62
À la carte 100-350FF,
menu 85-150FF

Mitsuko
8, Rue du Sabot, 75006
☎ 01 42 22 17 74
À la carte 120FF, menu 60-180FF

Russian

Chez Marianne
2, Rue des Hospitalières-
Saint-Gervais, 75004
☎ 01 42 72 18 86
À la carte 55-95FF

Irotchka
73, Rue Léon-Frot, 75011
☎ 01 40 09 19 02
À la carte 150FF, menu 110FF

Maroussia
9, Rue de l'Éperon, 75006
☎ 01 43 54 87 50
À la carte 240FF, menu 80-160FF

The Islands

ANTILLES

La Créole
122, Blvd du
Montparnasse, 75014
☎ 01 43 20 62 12
🖷 01 42 79 94 39
À la carte 220FF, menu 130FF

RÉUNION

Aux Petits Chandeliers
62, Rue Daguerre, 75014

☎ 01 43 20 25 87
🖷 01 43 27 87 38
À la carte 120FF, menu 50-100FF

SEYCHELLES

Au Coco de Mer
34, Blvd Saint-Marcel,
75005
☎ 01 47 07 06 64
🖷 01 47 07 41 88
Menu 140-170FF

A few more. . .

ENGLISH

Bertie's
1, Rue Léo-Delibes,
75016
☎ 01 44 34 54 34
À la carte 260FF, menu 220FF

BRAZILIAN

Aquaréla do Brasil
16, Rue de Liancourt,
75014
☎ 01 43 22 21 31
À la carte 80-180FF,
menu 60-180FF

SPANISH

Casa Alcalde
117, Blvd de Grenelle,
75015
☎ 01 47 83 39 71
À la carte 200FF, menu 150FF

LEBANESE

Al-Farès
166, Blvd de Grenelle,
75015
☎ 01 47 83 54 38
À la carte 100FF, menu 55-125FF

SYRIAN

Feyrouz
8, Rue de Lourmel, 75015
☎ 01 45 78 07 02
🖷 01 45 78 07 41
À la carte 100-150FF,
menu 70-100FF

JEWISH

Pitchi Poï
7, Rue Caron, 75004
☎ 01 42 77 75 49
À la carte 80-100FF, menu 150FF

FOREIGN CUISIN